LOGISTICAL FULFILLMENT

MATERIAL FULFILLMENT

CULTURAL FULFILLMENT

EXHIBITION: FULFILLED

PREFACE
Ashley Bigham

Based on the eponymous symposium and exhibition, *Fulfilled: Architecture, Excess, and Desire* considers the role of architecture in a culture shaped by excessive manufacturing and assuagement of desire. Until the term became synonymous with Amazon warehouses, the concept of fulfillment described the achievement of a desire—sometimes tangible, often psychological or spiritual. With the rapid growth of e-commerce, our understanding of fulfillment has evolved to reflect a seemingly endless cycle of desire and gratification—one whose continuity hinges on our willingness to overlook the cultural, economic, and environmental impacts of our ever-increasing expectation of quick and efficient fulfillment. A closer look at fulfillment reveals a social, typological, formal, aesthetic, and economic practice constructed collectively through both digital and physical interactions. It is a cultural practice which evolves like a language, both universally transferable and contextually specific. As a symposium, exhibition, and now publication, this project aims to draw out these new arrangements, sticky relationships, and material byproducts of cultural production and to ask again the age-old question, "What does it mean to be fulfilled?"

This book examines the architecture of fulfillment through three lenses: logistical, material, and cultural fulfillment. Each reveals the new forms of architectural practice and research that are possible, typical, and even surreptitiously encouraged in the age of Amazon. Fulfillment networks are not invisible systems; they are tangible objects—warehouses, suburban houses, parking lots, cardboard boxes, shopping malls, mechanical systems, shipping containers—with which architects necessarily interact. From political mapping and questions of labor to digital and physical storage typologies, contemporary architects learn from and work critically within the architecture of fulfillment. Their interests and approaches include the material and environmental shortcomings of global logistics and the formal, representational, and cultural potentials of a culture of excess. This book highlights architecture's unique capacity to offer methodologies for confronting an increasingly ambiguous, alienating world and produce new knowledge and unexpected solutions that go beyond the dichotomies of rural and urban territories.

Logistical fulfillment presents designs informed by global networks and distribution environments. From the initial inclination to the final object procurement, this section explores the myriad physical and digital environments that sustain the culture of fulfillment. Dramatic changes occurring in the production and procurement of global goods are shaping the types of architecture and spaces created. Architectural environments constitute the front- and back-ends of logistical fulfillment, from the living room laptop where items are browsed, reviewed, and purchased to the warehouses where objects are stored, stocked, and categorized.

Material fulfillment explores the use of materials as elements of global capital, finite resources, and aesthetic artifacts, probing the physical matter of fulfillment. As shown in this section, designers are as interested in distinguishing cultural attitudes toward the use of a material as they are in considering the physical properties of individual materials themselves. This group of designers works to elicit the latent potentials found in the materials of fulfillment networks. While many of these materials are mass produced and standardized across political contexts, their use and inevitable reuse are culturally specific.

Cultural fulfillment examines the architecture of desire through the proliferation of designed objects, from spoons to cities. Beyond the material and logistical aspects of fulfillment, cultural fulfillment presents a more complicated and potentially more rewarding aspect: the satisfaction of desire. In a supply chain where each box contains a scan code, and each meter of the delivery path is mapped for efficiency, there is something increasingly inefficient, yet absolutely necessary, about desire—its creation, and its effects on the world. *Fulfilled* posits the notion that all architecture is the result of desire—for space, shelter, beauty. Fulfillment, in this way, brings together the tangible nature of material production and the ineffable satisfaction of personal desire, and proposes that design is a necessary intangible in an increasingly tangible world.

ON FULFILLMENT
Ana Miljački

The term "fulfillment," especially in its noun form, is perhaps a lot like happiness, "a word that does things," a kindred, "hopeful performative."[1] But if you look it up online, via that old friend Google search (as I admit I did), you will find that Merriam-Webster offers two recent web usages of "fulfillment." The word was first employed in the year 1624; both demonstrations of its contemporary 2020 uses refer to fulfillment centers, particularly Amazon's and Best Buy's fulfillment centers in the age of coronavirus.[2] One sample paragraph refers to nearly 20,000 workers in fulfillment centers contracting the virus; the other describes how shopping patterns remained strong, a reality made possible, it is easy to infer, by the persistence of those thousands of infected workers, along with orange Kiva, Pegasus, and Xanthus robots, AI, and the postal service.

Though the coronavirus had already migrated from business class to economy, catching shorter, regional rides as we gathered in Columbus, Ohio for the *Fulfilled* symposium in February of 2020, it was not explicitly or self-consciously on the symposium agenda, though it was not far from it either. By design and word choice, *Fulfilled* intertwined material desires (maybe even hopes for happiness) and the vast logistical landscapes and protocols of delivering goods and services along some of the same routes the virus was traveling: beginning at open-air markets and crossing territories, moving via intimate encounters and bodily fluids to personal devices and eventually to the private rooms in which online orders are made, and continuing to others where wrist clicks are captured for the sake of machine learning, and the eventual production of predictive consumer patterns.[3] These predictive consumer patterns in turn literally organize stuff at fulfillment centers, and might eventually customize our own online interfaces, maybe even influencing production down the line.

And then back to the beginning. The work assembled for the *Fulfilled* symposium—and now its eponymous book—renders the capitalocene we inhabit as haunting and hauntingly delightful at times (I say this using my frayed resistance nerve endings to acknowledge that I am being worked on by all kinds of busy algorithms all the time). In drawing attention to aspects of our capitalocene, the symposium highlighted greater and lesser amounts of cognitive dissonance between the local and global logistics we participate in—simply by occupying this historical moment—and whose logics might govern not only their own fulfillment (as some logistical conclusion), but our own individual and collective sense of it as well.

We began the symposium by training our eyes on Keith Krumwiede's kaleidoscopic, obsessive house and subdivision plans, each a logical, satirical conclusion to a composite image of the little (developer) houses on the hillside and the "founding fathers'" white, slave-owning, settler, colonial dream of "equal opportunity" in Freedomland.[4] These set the tone for the event, which, though rendered in the post-millennial-pink vibrant multicolor, was about life and death—literally, and also about the life and death of architecture. On top of Freedomland's critical rumination on architecture's

---

1 See Sara Ahmed, *The Promise of Happiness* (Durham and London: Duke University Press, 2010).
2 Visited on October 6, 2020, https://www.merriam-webster.com/dictionary/fulfillment.
3 I refer here to Curtis Roth's presentation and research on wrist and gaze tracking data.
4 Keith Krumwiede showed us work that is part of his architectural fiction about Freedomland, compiled in his book *Atlas of Another America* (Zurich: Park Books, 2016).

complicity and agency, as part of the coda for our gathering, Ashley Bigham offered a kind of subversive "stickyness":[5] architecture that might be improvised, against the grain, illicit; that might be hard to compute; that might resist the contemporary systemic predation on privacy, even as it leaves loads of data in its wake. So, I made it a game for myself to track (like some fallible, all-too-human, counterpart to the AI-trained eye-wrist coordination predictor) how each of the presentations and bodies of work for which they advocated crossed and minded the gap between the automatism of expectations and their fulfillment and the messy unpredictability of life.

From Curtis Roth's mesmerizing, algorithmic, collectively authored paintings to Laida Aguire's estranged and vibrant off-the-shelf assemblies; from the urgency of Cristina Goberna's difficult sin complexes to Ashley Bigham's world-stitching, bottom-up market weaves; from improved everyday lives to improved everyday deaths, the work presented in *Fulfilled* unflinchingly assesses the contemporary ways of the capitalocene. Every project cracks open our complex and compromised world to unveil unexpected territories for aesthetic expression and architectural projects. This is architecture for the post-orthographic, the post-Net, the post-natural, the post-individual, the global, statistical, contemporary political and cultural moment. Some of it may even be ready for the pandemic and the post-pandemic era. I found the form of (perhaps we need to call it) realism these projects offered to be hopeful, even optimistic. Such is the effect of truth in the post-truth era, and yet optimism itself, of any kind, does not seem congruous with those very glimpses of our and architecture's predicament. Still, emboldened by the prospect of facing the music, of contemplating what architecture has to offer or might have to become given that "music," I offer two observations on the posture of the work included in the symposium and this book.

En masse, these bodies of work and practices perform a precarious balancing act. Not unlike the way "fulfillment" balances on a razor edge between pleasure and logistics, tangible experiences and the invisible violence of AI, these projects present dire prospects for architecture, and then—in a feat of hopeful realism—insist on a contribution through architecture. These days (just as in the days before COVID-19), a cursory scan across the headlines is enough to send one down a dark and lonely spiral. But the scholars and archi-

---

5 Ashley Bigham used "sticky" in this way in her live symposium introduction, which launched the two-day event at the Knowlton School of Architecture.

tects assembled here seem to look down that spiral, take its measure, and adjust the course forward. Bruno Latour advocated for a similar prospective posture in his "Attempt at a 'Compositionist Manifesto.'"[6] In Latour's 2010 essay and lecture, he "repainted" Paul Klee's famous *Angelus Novus* (1920). Klee's angel of history looks backward, and in fleeing forward in terror from what he sees, he tautologically proceeds to wreak the very havoc that terrifies him. Latour proposed that in response to this modernist conception of progress we might need to imagine ourselves looking forward with an eye to our collective prospects—which we might end up shaping, if we are lucky, organized, ingenious, or, more likely, all of the above.

Let me try another characterization of this prospective view: insofar as one can speak generally about the work assembled under *Fulfilled*, it offered a particularly contemporary flavor of irony. I did just characterize the very choice of forward-looking realism as a form of optimism, but it may be useful to complicate that idea a bit via Timothy Morton's concept of hyperobjects.[7] Climate crisis is Morton's primary hyperobject. It is so complex, so far beyond the scale of any single human life that it is hard to comprehend and even harder to "see." And yet, at its vast global and historical scale, we all perpetuate it through micro, individual acts of consumption and production. Morton describes a form of irony that is not the plastic, postmodern type, but rather the kind of irony conjured up in the presence of hyperobjects, which is to say, irony structural to the experience of reality. This paradoxically sincere irony couples self-awareness about the world with the realization that there is no distance to be had. Sincere irony in the presence of capitalocene's hyperobjects (climate crisis, white supremacy, statisticization of self, the patriarchy, or the finance-logistical complex) is like "being Jonah in the whale realizing that he is part of the whale's digestive system, or Han Solo and Leia inside the gigantic worm they think is the surface of an asteroid."[8] Sincere irony is not a trope, or an aesthetic device, it is woven into the very fabric of experience, it is the feeling of "waking up inside a hyperobject, against which we are always in the wrong."[9]

6 Bruno Latour, "An Attempt at a 'Compositionist Manifesto,'" *New Literary History* v. 41, N. 3, 2010: 471–90.
7 Timothy Morton, *Hyperobjects: Philosophy and Ecology after the End of the World* (Minneapolis: The University of Minnesota Press, 2013).
8 Morton, ibid., Part 2, "The Age of Asymmetry," paragraph 35.
9 Ibid.

Stickiness then may be key when inside the belly of a hyper-object. There used to be a time when a concept like "running room" for culture or criticality made sense. In an analog world, distinctions could be made between urns and chamber pots, between the utilitarian and the cultural.[10] If you have been a student of architecture at any point in the last two decades, you might have a lingering cultural memory of this type of running room. Hal Foster celebrated it not long ago, but it was put forward (in German as *Spielraum*) by satirist, poet, and publisher Karl Krauss as a way of describing a space in which cultural action could take place.[11] By running room, Krauss referred to a space produced by distinctions between high and low culture, between art and commerce, where various forms of creative imagination could play out with relative autonomy and from which their products could affect other dimensions of culture and life. It is a space or a concept, like many others, that we can now see as not only no longer available in the same way, but also as having only ever been a mental construct. From within the belly of hyperobjects, running room will at best seem like a quaint idea, and may need to be replaced by stickiness, while aesthetic and political agency could only be fragmentary, experimental, desiring, and self aware. Not bad. Though will it be enough to truly disrupt the inevitability of total fulfillment of the logistical and automatic type?

Indeed "What does it mean to be fulfilled"—but not in terms of the logics of the logistical, material, or cultural spheres?[12] What if we instead asked if political commitment could also offer a form of fulfillment as well as belonging? And how might this in turn change our odds against the hyperobjects in whose bellies we recognize ourselves to be? To go there, I follow the work of political theorist Jodi Dean, who has been theorizing the logic of "circulatory capitalism" as well as of crowds and the organizational structures on the left: the political party.[13] She recently offered a term "communicative capitalism" in order to further specify the contemporary effects of that circulatory capitalism.[14] Under communicative capitalism everyone and everything contributes to the constantly streaming flow of data and

10 Karl Krauss qtd. in Hall Foster, "The ABCs of Contemporary Design," *October*, v. 100, *Obsolescence* (Spring 2002): 196.
11 See Hal Foster, *Design and Crime* (London: Verso, 2002): 16.
12 "What does it mean to be fulfilled?" is the final sentence of the joint *Fulfilled* symposium and exhibition blurb. See https://knowlton.osu.edu/events/2020/02/fulfilled-exhibition.
13 See Jodi Dean, *Comrade: An Essay on Political Belonging* (London: Verso, 2019).
14 Jodi Dean, "Communicative Capitalism: Circulation and the Foreclosure of Politics," *Cultural Politics* 1 (March 2005): 51–74.

voices. Its chief characteristic is the fundamental separation of politics that circulate as "content" from politics as policy, or as real transformation. As messages are generated and consumed at greater and greater velocity, their "exchange value" eclipses their "use value," and they increasingly contribute only to their own flow, thus shifting the experience of activism from actually engaged and transformative acts to a vague sense of contribution (to that stream of commentary). In order to begin to assemble radical imagination in this context (which I believe is necessary), mutual interests or even "shared concerns" are not enough. Dean offers comradeship (over alliance or friendship) as a unique social and political bond, and the only one capable of standing up to communicative capitalism with other agendas, and in order to affect outcomes that might oppose it.

The projects and practices included in *Fulfilled* acknowledge and work with the social and technological "limits and fragility of the worlds we inhabit," which makes the individual contributions here urgent and transformative.[15] As you begin to engage them in this book, I leave you with a question that the *Fulfilled* symposium left me with, a question that seems only more pressing now: Would it be possible—and how would it change the work (your work) and its forms of agency—to place and articulate political goals outside of that work, such that all future gatherings of architects become gatherings of comrades set on transforming the discipline and the world together? Can we imagine collectively producing a program of action that might bind us to transformative goals beyond our own singular projects? These contributors' vulnerable hopefulness for the role of architecture in that transformation might be a good place to start.

15 Steven J. Jackson, "Rethinking Repair," in Tarleton Gillespie, Pablo J. Boczkowski, and Kirsten A. Foot, eds. *Media Technologies: Essays on Communication, Materiality, and Society* (Cambridge: MIT Press, 2014): 221.

FOREWORD
Keith Krumwiede

Fulfillment, in this Amazon age of algorithms and artificial intelligence, is increasingly synonymous with the streamlined logistics networks that quickly and efficiently deliver ever more stuff directly to the doors of increasingly impatient consumers. Still, there remains something in the idea of fulfillment that speaks to our human needs and desires as they might be liberated from our consumer selves. After a year in COVID-19 limbo, sequestered away from others and the viral threat that they (and we) pose, that notion of fulfillment seems more and more elusive. Denied the pleasures of assembly, of sharing physical space and not just digital time with others, fulfillment itself remains literally out of reach.

Architecture is a practice premised on fulfillment, grounded as it is in providing for fundamental human needs (for shelter, for order) and satisfying, and indeed stoking, human desires (for beauty, for power). The rewards of architecture, however, are not evenly distributed. The forms through which the discipline delivers fulfillment are all too frequently reserved for a select few. So, while the planet is littered with monuments, both beautiful and banal, to power and privilege, the dreams of architecture's better angels have gone largely unfulfilled.

In the face of political and market forces that aim to subjugate us and our desires, what would it mean today to practice architecture as a form of fulfillment for all? In orienting us toward the systems of relations that shape the world, the projects collected in *Fulfilled* offer some direction. These architects are not intent on adding more monuments, more forms, more things, to the world; they are concerned instead with how we relate to the things in the world and to one another through those things. They tell us that an architecture of fulfillment would focus more on relationships than on form; that it would seek to stage arenas of mutual responsibility and shared action, settings in which people gather and, should their desires align, fulfill one another.

The practices mapped out across these pages do not follow well-worn paths toward known, seemingly comforting ends. They evade the neoliberal demand that architecture provide a quantifiable service supplying products to feed the fulfillment market. A service of another kind is offered here: one that rewires existing networks of fulfillment to engender instead a system of reciprocal bonds of care-giving and care-taking. In this view, fulfillment, when achieved, is not selfish but mutual. The offerings that follow—and they should be seen as such—bend our understanding of fulfillment away from the satisfaction of personal desire or consumer need and toward a condition of complementary care, shared sadness, and perhaps even polyphonic joy. There is, in this work, the promise of a world in which fulfillment is available to all.

CONTRIBUTOR
BIOGRAPHIES

ASHLEY BIGHAM is co-director of Outpost Office and an assistant professor at the Knowlton School of Architecture at The Ohio State University. She has been a Fulbright Fellow in Ukraine, a MacDowell Fellow, and a Walter B. Sanders Fellow at the University of Michigan's Taubman College of Architecture and Urban Planning. Her writing and work have appeared in publications such as *MAS Context, Metropolis, Mark, CLOG,* and *Surface.* The design work of Outpost Office has been exhibited at the Milwaukee Art Museum, the Tallinn Architecture Biennale, the Chicago Architecture Biennial, Roca London Gallery, Wedge Gallery, Yale School of Architecture, Princeton School of Architecture, Harvard GSD, and The Cooper Union.

LLUÍS ALEXANDRE CASANOVAS BLANCO is a New York- and Madrid-based architect, curator, and scholar. His design work has been recognized with several prizes, including the Simon Architecture Prize 2018 and the Bauwelt Prize 2019. He was also a finalist for the Lisbon Triennale Millennium bcp Début Award 2019 for architects under 35. He was the chief curator of the Oslo Architecture Triennale 2016 together with the After Belonging Agency and has recently co-curated the show *Invisible Auto Sacramental* at MNCA Reina Sofía, Madrid. He has been a fellow in several institutions, including the Whitney Independent Study Program and the IKKM-Weimar Princeton Summer School for Media Studies. He is currently a PhD Candidate at Princeton University.

MICHELLE CHANG directs JaJa Co and teaches architectural design at Harvard GSD. She founded her independent practice in 2014 after working in offices in New York, Boston, and San Francisco. Her design work experiments with the overlaps between and among film, installation, music, teaching, and building. Chang is a former MacDowell Fellow, Wortham Fellow, and a recipient of the Architectural League Prize for Young Architects + Designers. In her research, she studies the techniques and histories of architectural representation. Specifically, she investigates how optics, digital media, and modes of cultural production influence translations between design and building.

CURRENT INTERESTS is a Los Angeles-based architectural design studio founded by Matthew Au and Mira Henry. As a creative collaboration, Current Interests' built work is grounded in notions of material specificity, color relationships, assembly details, and an engagement in critical cultural thinking. Matthew and Mira are design faculty at Southern California Institute for Architecture and have visiting faculty appointments at Princeton University and Harvard Graduate School of Design.

Matthew's academic work is deeply influenced by the history of conceptual art practice as he examines the spaces and tools of production, and the lines of communication that connect the worlds of design and building. He holds a Bachelor in Studio Art and Art History from the University of California, San Diego, and a Master of Architecture from Southern California Institute of Architecture. Mira's formal research and writing focus on architecture, race, and materiality. She is the recipient of the 2019 Architectural League

Prize, Henry Adams AIA Award, and Archiprix International Gold Medal. Mira holds a Bachelor in Art History from the University of Chicago and a Master of Architecture from UCLA.

LEIGHA DENNIS is a designer and educator based in New York. Her practice investigates the impact of digital technology and network culture on architecture and the built environment. Leigha is co-director of the Network Architecture Lab and a design director in the design studio 2x4, where she leads environmental projects at the intersection of architecture, branding, and storytelling. Leigha was previously a Muschenheim Fellow at the University of Michigan and a Fellow in Architecture at the Akademie Schloss Solitude. Her work has been shown at notable institutions including the New Museum, Museum of Modern Art, and Contemporary Art Centre in Vilnius. She holds degrees in architecture from the University of Michigan and Columbia University.

MILES GERTLER is an artist and co-founder of Common Accounts, which he directs with Igor Bragado. Their projects have considered the design of death and the virtual afterlife, including *Three Ordinary Funerals*, a prototypical funeral home produced for the 2017 Seoul Biennale of Architecture and Urbanism, now in the permanent collection of the MMCA, Seoul. Gertler and Bragado have contributed to publications such as *PIN-UP, e-flux, 032c,* and *FRAME Magazine*. Recent exhibitions include *Greater Toronto Art 2021* at MOCA (Toronto); *Redesign Death* at the Cube Museum, Kerkrade (2020); *Working Remotely* at a83, New York (2020); *Age of You*, curated by Shumon Basar, Douglas Coupland, Hans Ulrich Obrist for MOCA (Toronto) in 2019; *Aging World* at the Seoul Museum of Art (2019); and *Going Fluid* at the 3rd Istanbul Design Biennial (2016).

CRISTINA GOBERNA PESUDO is a New York- and Barcelona-based architect, critic, educator, and founder of Fake Industries Architectural Agonism, Epic Architecture, and The Destitute Institute. Through buildings, text, photography, theater, and pedagogy, her work explores the potential of agonism and epic theater to unveil issues normally overlooked by the architectural field. She is a PhD candidate at the European Graduate School in Switzerland in the Department of Philosophy, Art, and Critical Thought and in the ETSAB in Barcelona, where she is writing a dissertation about the Architecture of Desire.

After teaching at Columbia GSAPP, Sydney UTS, MIT, and Cooper Union, she is currently a visiting lecturer at the Royal College of Art in London and a professor at BAU Escola de Disseny in Barcelona.

KEITH KRUMWIEDE, author of *Atlas of Another America*, is a professor and Dean of Architecture at the California College of the Arts. In 2018 he was the Arnold W. Brunner/Katherine Edwards Gordon Rome Prize Fellow in Architecture at the American Academy in Rome.

JESSE LECAVALIER is principal of LECAVALIER R+D and associate professor at the Cornell University College of Architecture, Art, and Planning. LeCavalier uses the tools of urban design and architecture to research, theorize, and speculate about infrastructure. He is the author of *The Rule of Logistics: Walmart and the Architecture of Fulfillment* (University of Minnesota Press, 2016). Projects include *Shelf Life* for the 2018 MoMA PS1 Young Architects Program, *Intentional Estates Agency* (with Tei Carpenter, Dan Taeyoung, and Chris Woebken) for the 2019 Oslo Triennale, and *Architectures of Fulfillment* for the 2017 Seoul Biennale.

ANG LI is an assistant professor at the School of Architecture at Northeastern University. She is the founder of Ang Li Projects, a research-centered design practice that operates at the intersection of architecture, experimental preservation, and public art to explore the maintenance rituals and material afterlives behind architectural production. Her work has been featured in numerous exhibitions, including the 2013 Lisbon Architecture Triennale, the 2019 Chicago Architecture Biennial, and Exhibit Columbus 2020-2021. Ang holds a Master of Architecture from Princeton University and a Bachelor of Arts in architecture from the University of Cambridge.

JOHN MCMORROUGH is an architect who writes about culture and design methods, with a focus on architecture's extended field (buildings, but also complementary media, such as images, installations, and other structured narratives). His writing and design work have appeared in publications such as *Perspecta, Log, Threshold, MAS Context,* and *Flat Out.* He has taught theory and design at the Yale School of Architecture, The Ohio State University, the University of Applied Arts Vienna, and the Graduate School of Design at Harvard

University, among other institutions, and he is currently an associate professor at the Taubman College of Architecture and Urban Planning at the University of Michigan.

ANA MILJAČKI is a critic, curator, and Associate Professor of Architecture at MIT, where she teaches history, theory, and design. In addition, she directs the Critical Broadcasting Lab at MIT. She was part of the three-member curatorial team, with Eva Franch i Gilabert and Ashley Schafer, of the US Pavilion at the 2014 Venice Architecture Biennale, where their project, OfficeUS, critically examined the last century of US architects' global contribution. Miljački is the author of *The Optimum Imperative: Czech Architecture for the Socialist Lifestyle 1938–1968* (Routledge, 2017), co-editor of the OfficeUS series of books, guest editor of *Praxis 14: True Stories*, and editor of *Terms of Appropriation: Modern Architecture and Global Exchange* with Amanda Reeser Lawrence (Routledge, 2018) as well as *The Under the Influence* symposium proceedings (Actar, 2019).

CURTIS ROTH is an associate professor at the Knowlton School of Architecture at The Ohio State University. He was previously a resident fellow at the Akademie Schloss Solitude in Stuttgart, and a partner of OfficeUS. He holds a Master of Architecture from the Massachusetts Institute of Technology. His research examines new formations of subjectivity within networks of computation, labor, and distance.

STOCK-A-STUDIO is an architectural design practice with equal interests in the scenographic and the utilitarian. Their research links material resources to the immaterial systems that proliferate and qualify them: from product catalogs, to assembly methods, to the influence of aesthetics in the circular economy. stock-a-studio's work is often physical and often digital, more often both. Their projects have been commissioned by Superblue Miami, Berghain Club, Storefront for Art and Architecture, A+D Museum, Queer camps, Berlin Art Week, Milan Architecture Week, and Oya Music Festival. LAIDA AGUIRRE, founder of stock-a-studio, is an assistant professor at the University of Michigan's Taubman College of Architecture and Urban Planning.

LOGISTICAL FULFILLMENT

CLOUDS
Leigha Dennis

To have and not to have, to own and to crave,
finally collapsed in a single emotion.
—Rem Koolhaas, *Junkspace* (Quodlibet, 2006): 151.

Clouds is a photo essay that documents the self-storage industry as cloud storage for domestic objects. If digital clouds provide data storage with remote servers, then aren't self-storage facilities the analog clouds for our homes?

I took this series of photographs between New York, New York and Ann Arbor, Michigan in 2014, a time when images of data centers were popular in the media and were becoming a kind of aestheticized space.

I was interested in these storage facilities as an embodiment of the American Dream, with the American single-family home being territory for the domestication of postwar technology. The structure of the home itself is prefabricated, duplicated, and commodified—replete with televisions, coffee tables, and dishwashers. Consumerism fueled the commercialization of domesticity. Between 1960 and 2000, household consumption increased by 400%, and homes were bursting at the seams.

We love our stuff. We hate our stuff. We dream of being free of it. We purge for the cathartic impression of control, the quest to find order in entropy, keeping email inboxes at zero and routinely cleaning the refrigerator. Yet, many of us own more objects than we realize. The objects are ambient, contributing to the atmospheres of our homes. They represent past relationships and hold un-tapped potential. They possess histories and stories, some nostalgic and some banal, just meaningful enough to keep them around. Ultimately, it is easier to house excess possessions remotely at a nearby storage facility than to discard them. In turn, the home can appear tidy and pure.

CLOUDS — DENNIS

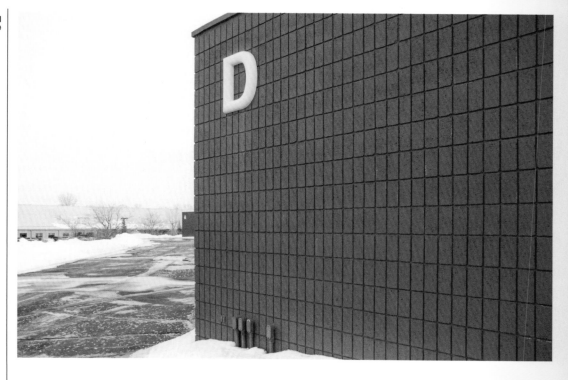

But even in economic downturns, households continue to acquire more objects, and now the 39-billion-dollar self-storage industry services one in every 10 American households.[1] Though self-storage is one of the few real estate sectors that has proven to be recession-proof, the COVID-19 pandemic has shaken the industry somewhat, as Americans have largely ceased moving, and local governments have placed moratoriums on rental evictions.

1 Mooallem, Jon. "The Self-Storage Self." In *The New York Times*. September 2, 2009.
http://www.nytimes.com/2009/09/06/magazine/06self-storage-t.html?pagewanted=all&_r=0ˆ.

Ultimately, we know that many people use storage facilities when they lose their homes to foreclosure, get evicted, or have to downsize for economic reasons. These spaces come to represent larger systemic problems, such as access to housing and decent employment. One of the reasons I took these photographs was to depict the architecture of foreclosure that wasn't the typical boarded up house with plywood in the windows; these images represent stagnant pasts and latent futures.

A version of this essay was originally published in ARPA Journal, Issue 02, The Search Engine, November 18, 2014: arpaournal.net/clouds-2.

CLOUDS — DENNIS

NATURES OF FULFILLMENT
Jesse LeCavalier

⋀ Herman Hartwich, *View of the Hackensack Meadows with Jersey City in the Distance* (1870). Oil on canvas, 10 ¼ x 21 ½ in. Courtesy of the Middlebury College Museum of Art, Vermont.

Herman Hartwich's painting, *View of the Hackensack Meadows with Jersey City in the Distance* (1870), is notable for the vastness and openness of the landscape it depicts. Clouds drift through a blue sky and a river meanders through largely untouched terrain. The end of the Palisades Escarpment is visible on the horizon along with Jersey City and, though we cannot see it, we know Manhattan is there as well. In the years immediately following the American Civil War, New York City was establishing itself as the commercial and shipping hub of the region. Several different Hudson County municipalities had just been consolidated into Greater Jersey City with major railroad terminals soon to follow. These were key transfer points for goods flowing east and for immigrants heading west through Ellis Island. Thus, Hartwich's otherwise unremarkable landscape is activated by the railroad leading from the left of the frame to the central horizon. Now called the Northeast Corridor Line, the railway makes itself known through multiple plumes of smoke indexing the active movement of goods and people. In the latter 19th century, such plumes were signs of progress and an emerging modernity (mastery of transport being one of the decisive features of the Union Army) and not the signs of industrial pollution and catastrophic climate change as they might register to an audience in the early 21st century. Even so, a remarkable thing about this image is how little, indeed, has changed. The Meadowlands, as the area is now known, remains surprisingly vast and open, riven with rail lines and industry; it is essentially a landscape of fulfillment—a key point of interchange between goods, people, energy, information, and waste. In what follows, I consider some of the ways the Meadowlands has been imagined and reimagined and argue that its qualities emerge through its role as a logistical landscape.

TOXIC WORK ENVIRONMENT

Located across the Hudson River from Manhattan, the Meadowlands exists in the popular imagination today as a tantalizing metaphor but is also, more significantly, an active and populated place full of people working, playing, or otherwise living their lives. For example, the title sequence of television series *The Sopranos* presents the Meadowlands as the beginning of a progression from grim reality to fantasies of domestic retreat, while also suggesting the tenacity of that reality. The Meadowlands—as a regional eco-urban-infrastructural entanglement—comprises a network of wetlands and waterways, including the lower Passaic and Hackensack rivers as well as a host of industrial and infrastructural installations. From the beginning of colonial occupation of the region, the Meadowlands has been treated as a service landscape.[1] In the 20th century its cheap land prices and perceived lack of environmental value made it a desirable home for major industrial concerns. And while the industries that made the Meadowlands one of the most polluted sites in the country have largely departed or shut down, the area remains an active logistical zone. Logistics is a metabolic industry that manages a series of inputs, outputs, and exchanges, including waste, energy, data, food, and consumer products; it weaves itself into the landscape in often invisible ways and, in the process, further transforms an already deeply altered place.

Scientific American, "Diking and Draining the New Jersey Meadows" Vol. 19 No. 5 (July 29, 1868). Public Domain.

While the Meadowlands region is full of aquatic life, the state prohibits consumption of fish or shellfish from the Lower Passaic River and Newark Bay.[2] This is not because the populations are dwindling but because rivers are so contaminated with dioxin that the fish are unsafe for humans to eat. During the middle of the 20th century, the Meadowlands was a center of DDT production and the pairing of 2,4,5-trichlorophenoxyacetic acid with 2,4-dichlorophenoxyacetic acid to create Agent Orange, whose wanton use during the Vietnam War caused significant destruction and suffering. Diamond Alkali was the primary producer of this chemical and one of the most active polluters in the area. With the discovery of astonishingly high amounts of dioxin in the soil and groundwater, production was suspended and containment efforts were initiated under the Comprehensive Environmental Response, Compensation, and Liability Act of 1980 (CERCLA), otherwise known as the "Superfund Program." In pursuit of corporate accountability, the Superfund program is administered by the EPA. Sites are designated as "superfund" sites and placed on a national priorities list. From there, the EPA pursues parties

1 Robert Sullivan, *The Meadowlands: Wilderness Adventures at the Edge of a City* (New York: Anchor, 1999).
2 "Fish Smart Eat Smart NJ," State of New Jersey Department of Environmental Projection, accessed April 4, 2021, https://www.nj.gov/dep/dsr/njmainfish.htm. Anchor, 1999).

Popular Science Monthly, "A Magic City from a Swamp" (October 1928). Public Domain.

Regional Plan Association, "A Glimpse of the Industrial Section of the Proposed Hackensack Meadows Development," *Regional Plan of New York and its Environs, Volume II: Building of the City* (1931), 541. Courtesy of Regional Plan Association.

responsible for the contamination in order to compel them to contribute funding for remediation efforts. As it is structured to hold polluters accountable, efforts to recuperate funding to restore sites are often thwarted because the polluters cannot be identified or located. As of 2020, the site remains unready for reuse or redevelopment.[3]

The Diamond Alkali (also known as Diamond Shamrock, after a 1967 merger with Shamrock Oil Company) site is one of many Superfund sites in the Meadowlands, including a substantial cluster around Berry's Creek. Because of the challenges of holding polluting parties accountable, land remediation efforts can be slow and costly. As a result, the Superfund Program tends to act as a default preservation mechanism by banking land in sites that can neither be developed nor remediated. The contaminated conditions are exacerbated by the area's high water table and vulnerability to weather events like Hurricane Sandy. The Rebuild by Design program (RBD) proposed a suite of strategic and systemic infrastructure transformations, such as integrated forms of urban development and stormwater management. However, such transformations operate at a different pace than the current rhythms of the site. Many developers and land holders adopted more localized responses to environmental vulnerabilities, including raising slab heights above the flood plain or constructing landscape barriers around their complexes. These responses are effective locally but succeed at the potential expense of the larger region through, for example, the addition of impermeable surfaces. The marshes of the Meadowlands have their own controversial way of managing the effects of climate change: *Phragmites australis*, also known as the common reed.

3 "Superfund Site: Diamond Alkali Co., Newark, NJ," United States Environmental Protection Agency, accessed April 4, 2021, https://cumulis.epa.gov/supercpad/CurSites/csitinfo.cfm?id=0200613&msspp=med.

TERRAFORMLESS

Over the past century, the Meadowlands has been a site of significant Phragmites expansion. Understood as a rampant non-native
species, Phragmites beds produce dynamics that accelerate its own
monocultural growth, including a dense sun-blocking biomass as
well as toxins that result from its decomposition.[4] At the same time,
studies are currently investigating whether the large networks of
the plant could help mitigate flood damage or act as a carbon sink.[5]
Human intervention catalyzed the rampant growth of Phragmites
by continued efforts to "drain the swamp," as it were, by developers
convinced there was money to be made in these locations. An illus-
tration from the July 29, 1868 issue of *Scientific American* depicts a
scene of a monumental earthwork under construction. The illustra-
tion, titled *Diking and Draining the New Jersey Meadows*, depicts the

use of a patented technology by Spencer
B. Driggs for "Improvement in Dikes and
Levees to Rivers." In the lower right of the
image, teams of men position and pound
iron plates into the marshy soil. Further
to the left, crewmen transfer soil from the
temporary embankment to the more permanent one in progress. As the soil is built up
around the plate, the top of the mound is
leveled and the sloping sides stabilized. In the
distance, figures are walking along the top of
the newly finished levee and beyond them, a
paddle steamer makes its way along the water.

▲ Regional Plan Association, "Design for Entrance to
the Future Civic and Business Center of the Meadows
City from the Basin at the Head of the Proposed
Hackensack River Straightening," *Regional Plan of
New York and its Environs, Volume II: Building of the City*
(1931), 543. Courtesy of Regional Plan Association.

In the foreground, posh-looking fellows survey the scene. The juxta-
position of these men with the scores of workmen undertaking back-
breaking labor invokes imperial images of the past: indeed the tenor
of the enterprise was in the "conquering" of the unruly marsh. The
attending article describes how:

> such lands are not only unproductive of anything which can
> observe any important purpose, but they are productive of

4 Peter Deltredici, *Wild Urban Plants of the Northeast: A Field Guide* (Ithaca: Cornell University
Press, 2010).
5 "Phragmites: Questions and Answers," US Fish and Wildlife Service, Accessed April 7, 2021,
https://www.fws.gov/GOMCP/pdfs/phragmitesQA_factsheet.pdf; for one of several studies of
phragmites and its consequences, see for example: Kai Whitaker, et al., "Vegetation persistence
and carbon storage: Implications for environmental water management for Phragmites australis"
Water Resource Research, June 2015, https://doi.org/10.1002/2014WR016253.

numerous evils. Teeming with miasmas, the home of mischievous and annoying insects, they are blotches upon the otherwise fair face of nature. To render them fruitful, and productive of good rather than evil, is a problem for which a solution has been anxiously sought, but heretofore only partially obtained.[6]

Driggs's invention is held up as this solution, in part for its understanding of the problem in section, i.e., that one must operate above and below the soil to make any significant impact on the "reclamation" process.

The possibilities of a Meadowlands that was rendered "fruitful and productive" continued to animate regional planning discussions, including the Regional Plan Association's First Report from 1928. The report includes an outlandish plan for a city of a million people. The ensuing plan is a web of superimposed systems and the product of a collision between the boulevards and axes typical of the City Beautiful movement with the contingencies of a landscape riven with transport right of ways. Rather than distorting the existing inconvenient infrastructures to fit the future plan, it instead obscures them through the overlay of similarly crisscrossing organizational elements. The plan matter-of-factly suggests straightening the Hackensack River to make room for a seaplane landing and a new kind of mini-Manhattan out of what is now Kearny Point. An accompanying article from *Popular Science* ("A Magic City from a Swamp") casually notes that the plan would require 200 million cubic yards of soil to raise the entire area 10 feet.[7] While the image of the RPA plan is more provocation than proposal; the detailed, *au courant* perspectives of Streamline Moderne facades and crisp International Style office buildings include what we would now call multimodal transfer points in which water, road, rail, and air intersect. Such imagery reinforces the primacy of transportation in the region. The RPA plan is a terraforming enterprise in which massive civil engineering work would effectively erase the landscape. However, the Meadowlands tends to have an entropic effect on such efforts. Its marshy ground and surprising wildness frustrate and disorganize efforts to contain it.

The stubbornly unbuildable landscape of the Meadowlands has continued to pose challenges for different forms of development. The pet food company Hartz was able to transform part of Secaucus

---

6 "Diking and Draining the New Jersey Meadows," *Scientific American* (July 29, 1868), 66.
7 "A Magic City from a Swamp," *Popular Science Monthly* (October 1928), 49.

into its current state of light industry and distribution landscape by recognizing the need for affordable land within striking distance of New York City. Across the river from Secaucus sits the better-known Meadowlands Sports Complex, next to which a new megamall has been sputtering to completion. Triple Five Worldwide, who also own Mall of America and West Edmonton Mall, are managing the project—called American Dream—and intend on making it one of the largest shopping and entertainment complexes in the country. Among other amenities, American Dream includes an indoor ski slope, an indoor water park, and an indoor NHL hockey rink. After years of planning and halting construction, American Dream had its soft opening in December 2019, just in time for visits to halt due to the COVID-19 pandemic.

In their promotional material, Triple Five generously estimates 40 million annual visitors, which is a Super Bowl's worth of people every day making their way, slowly, through the Meadowlands' frustrating circuits. Fifty years earlier, artist Robert Smithson famously made a similar journey by boarding a bus at the Port Authority and heading west. In his essay, "A Tour of the Monuments of Passaic, New Jersey," Smithson described the post-industrial landscape of the Meadowlands as being full of "ruins in reverse" and the area as "full of holes [which are] in a sense vacancies that define, without trying, the memory-traces of an abandoned set of futures."[8] American Dream is no exception to this, having languished for years under the name "Xanadu" as the failed first attempt to answer a question few were asking. During its dormancy, Xanadu's half-finished buildings were both monuments and ruins— a cautionary tale for builders and an elegy for the landscape they destroyed. Its monumentality notwithstanding, American Dream is one of many false futures enshrined in the Meadowlands.

LANDFILLS OF THE MEADOWLANDS
A Catalog of Local Infrastructure

1-B / RUTHERFORD LANDFILL 1-A / SKYMOUND MALANKA LANDFILL

ERIE LANDFILL AVON LANDFILL 1-D

KINGSLAND LANDFILL KEEGAN LANDFILL 1-E

Λ Landfills of the New Jersey Meadowlands. Jesse LeCavalier, *Natures of Logistics* (2019).

⋏ Minor infrastructures of the Meadowlands. Jesse LeCavalier, *Natures of Logistics* (2019).

⋏ Minor infrastructures of the Meadowlands. Jesse LeCavalier, *Natures of Logistics* (2019).

Smithson and his partner Nancy Holt, both originally from the area, are useful guides, conceptually and literally. While Smithson's *Monuments of Passaic* might be one of his most well-known projects, *Swamp* (a collaboration between both artists from 1971) conjures the atmosphere of the Meadowlands more viscerally. As Holt makes her way through the reeds, looking only through her camera's viewfinder, Smithson relays directions. Viewers share Holt's disorienting journey into the reeds as she tries to stay on high ground while Smithson urges her onward. In 1984, Holt developed *Skymound* for one of the capped landfills. The project uses the landscape's industrial history and orients it toward geomatic transcendence. Rather than erasing or reorganizing the ground, *Skymound* seems to embrace the impurity of the place. In the concessions it makes, the work connects to the arguments the Canadian philosopher Alexis Shotwell develops in *Against Purity*: "if we want a world with less suffering and more flourishing, it would be useful to perceive complexity and complicity as the constitutive situation of our lives, rather than as things we should avoid."[9] In this sense, the Meadowlands and our relationship to it is both complex and complicit. For those living in the region, the Meadowlands is a kind of shadow backyard, an infrastructural double that keeps the place going. It is a landscape mutually constructed by the logistical concerns that circulate through it and the entropic tendencies of the biological, ecological, and geological spheres.

NATURES OF LOGISTICS

At the same time, the Meadowlands is not some kind of smooth-running machine but rather the result of logistical processes—often abstracted as a set of balance sheets in some remote management office—colliding with the stubborn features of the landscape to create

8 Robert Smithson, "A Tour of the Monuments of Passaic, New Jersey." Originally published as "The Monuments of Passaic." *Artforum* 6, no.4 (December 1967), 55.
9 Alexis Shotwell, *Against Purity: Living Ethically in Compromised Times* (Minneapolis: University of Minnesota Press, 2016), 8.

a hybrid condition of environment, machine, and human. Seen from this perspective, one might ask how "nature" acts on logistics in the sense that the latter pursues control and mechanical efficiency above all else and the former tends to resist both. While a dialectic between the ordered space of logistics and the entropic forces of the Meadowlands emerges, the particular quality of the place stems from the persistent lack of resolution of this tension. American cultural theorist Sianne Ngai shows how the "sublime" aesthetics associated with dramatic and powerful forces of nature tend to conclude in some kind of cathartic resolution. Instead she explores the "suspended minor feelings" that attend this lack of synthesis, especially evident in what she describes as "the interesting" and the ease with which that category can drift into becoming "merely" interesting, i.e., boring.[10] It is precisely the Meadowlands' apparent boringness that offers both insight into the behavior of logistics and also the potential for infrastructure to engage such a place without asserting or insisting itself.

▲ Observation deck, soil processing, and future transit note at Universal Oil Products CERCLA Site. Jesse LeCavalier, *Natures of Logistics* (2020).

The Meadowlands is an unambiguously toxic site; decades of industrial negligence have turned the ground into a poison sponge. At the same time, the place is full of beauty and wonder, albeit maddeningly difficult to navigate. Centuries of development efforts, luckily, have failed because of a tendency to approach the area with a binary perspective. Efforts like RBD have popularized a "soft" approach to development that "works with" the landscape but does not necessarily question the need for development in the first place. Indeed, the fascination of the Meadowlands is in its resistance to imageability. As it has transformed, it has merged with the infrastructural layers such that it can be difficult to tell which is which. Landfills become habitats and pipeline berms create new marshland. Consum-

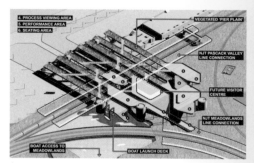

▲ Observation deck, soil processing, and future transit note at Universal Oil Products CERCLA Site. Jesse LeCavalier, *Natures of Logistics* (2020).

10 Sianne Ngai, *Our Aesthetic Categories: Zany, Cute, Interesting* (Cambridge: Harvard University Press, 2012), 134.

erist leisure complexes such as server farms and regional distribution centers proliferate. Polluted parcels ironically create new forms as multiple species find ways to make do. This logistical-natural co-construction of the Meadowlands tells a story about the larger global entanglements between the two. Attending to these dynamics can help find ways of working that understand and take seriously the needs of those (human and non-human) for whom and for which the Meadowlands is important without assuming or repeating familiar development logics.

As a complement to historical research into the Meadowlands, *Natures of Logistics* is a graphic documentation and speculative project about the potential of industrial vernacular to merge with in-site remediation efforts to create a series of "minor" infrastructures. By accepting the potential of its limited agency, distributed infrastructural installations can provide just enough repetitive recognition to give permission to explore, inhabit, and advocate for this place—as many already do. As this emergent collective language intersects with in situ remediation processes, new forms of nature emerge that are neither the sublime nature of wilderness nor the "tamed" nature of agriculture but a more unruly logistical nature that brings with it new landscapes, forms, and publics.

ANTHROPOFORMING, OR LIVING WITH OUR SELVES
Curtis Roth

∧   Painting produced with a software that allows online workers to exchange drawing labor for stock in a painting. Curtis Roth, *Stock Painting 1* (2020).

Perhaps it's best to begin with the Dolly Parton Challenge: a meme created sometime in late January 2020 that was fully dead by mid-March. First posted along with the caption "Get you a woman who can do it all" on Parton's Twitter feed, the meme consisted of a foursquare grid depicting the singer's dissimilar profile pictures for her hypothetical LinkedIn, Facebook, Instagram, and Tinder accounts.[1] But unlike most memes, Parton's was framed as a #challenge, calling on her audience to produce their own four-square iterations. If it's true that a post becomes a meme because an audience identifies a certain universality in its message, the resonance of Parton's meme over the following two months suggests the degree to which we already intuitively understand our lives as being comprised of incongruous self-presentations. Parton's problem of incongruous presentations turns out to be nearly as old as computers themselves. Before Alan Turing's eponymous Turing Test gauged the difference between humans and intelligent machines, it first imagined subjects on either end of a computer network trying to determine whether they were speaking with a woman or a man,[2] suggesting that even our earliest encounters with computation were premised on a cleaving of ourselves as flows of information circulating atop bodily substrates.[3] But while such multiplied presentations have perhaps always allowed us to navigate our public and private commitments, the usefulness of multiplying our self into selves has depended almost entirely on the strict segregation of such selves from one another. Parton's challenge, on the other hand, suggests that as we become entangled within the strange protocols of the platform economy, one's value not only depends on *doing it all*, but on making *doing it all* presentable in the process.

By way of an example, the reader might pause to examine their own Google Ad Personalization tab. Chances are good that when you opened your first Chrome browser window or signed up for a Gmail account, Google's profiling algorithm knew little more than your name, your age, and your gender identification. Today, your profile almost certainly contains thousands of characteristics ranging from your musical tastes to your shopping preferences, each

1 Christie D'Zurilla, "Dolly Parton created this meme and now celebs are in on the joke too," *Los Angeles Times*, January 24, 2020.
2 A. M. Turing, "Computing Machinery and Intelligence," *Mind*, Volume LIX, Issue 236, 1950.
3 Katherine N. Hayles, "How We Became Posthuman, Virtual Bodies in Cybernetics, Literature and Informatics," University of Chicago, 1999. Of the role of gender presentation in Turing's test, Hayles argues, "What Turing's test 'proves' is that the overlay between the enacted and the represented bodies is no longer a natural inevitability but a contingent production, mediated by a technology that has become so entwined with the production of identity that it can no longer meaningfully be separated from the human subject."

allowing Google Ads to more accurately predict your desires as you interact with the internet.[4] In 2013, Google introduced an updatable remarketing list, Similar Audiences. This list profiles each individual Google user through a minimum of a thousand data points generated by a user's previous behaviors and aggregates them into dynamic groups defined by specific similarities.[5] Crucially, Similar Audiences is not just a method for deriving a more accurate profile based on your past behaviors, but a method for accurately anticipating your profile to come.[6]

Such anticipatory forecasts are inferred from the millions of other lives encountered by the same algorithm simultaneously. For instance, Google might anticipate that your recent interest in gym memberships will soon be followed by an enthusiasm for dating. Romance will be preemptively added to your advertising profile in anticipation of the user that you're suddenly more likely to become. Just like the Queen of Nashville's "woman who can do it all," the more heterogeneous a Google user's various activities are, the more valuable their audience profile becomes. But while a highly specialized algorithm might not be necessary to draw a correlation between exercise and romance, systems like Google's Similar Audiences depend on advanced neural networks capable of predicting futures that simple correlational thinking could never envision. In 2015, an Uber executive revealed at a private party that their God View algorithm allows the company to reliably predict users' one-night stands through their transportation patterns.[7] Today, your "selves" not only multiply across individual online platforms, but proliferate into a near-infinite array of future selves made possible by an innovation in statistical thinking known as Bayes's Method.

First theorized by statistician Thomas Bayes and published posthumously in 1763, Bayes's theorem argued that the likelihood

4 Prior to 2018, Google Ads was known as AdWords.
5 "About Similar Audiences," Google Ads Help, https://support.google.com/google-ads/answer/7151628?hl=en. Accessed on July 28, 2019.
6 While the full functionality of Google's targeting algorithm is only available to advertisers who pay for the service, users can see a portion of this information through the "Ad Personalization" tab in their Google profile. My own contains 264 interests including Bollywood films, women's issues, coatings and adhesives, and flowers.
7 David Golumbia, Chris Gilliard, "There Are No Guardrails on Our Privacy Dystopia," *Motherboard*, March 10, 2018. In a since-deleted blog post on the company's website, Uber revealed a category of ride the company refers to as a "Ride-of-Glory," which entails a drop-off between 10pm and 4am, on a Friday or Saturday night, followed by a second ride 4–6 hours later within 1/10th of a mile from the original drop-off location. In 2014, the company began using this information to determine which cities had the most one-night stands per capita. See Jose Pagliery. "Uber removes racy blog posts on prostitution, one-night stands." *CNN Business*, November 25, 2014.

of an assertion being correct increases based on prior knowledge of conditions related to that assertion. While certainly not new, Bayesian analysis requires intensive calculation that often made it prohibitively inefficient until recent advances in computation. Over the last two decades, Bayes's Method has come to upend the dominant form of statistical prediction in the 20th century known as frequentism. To illustrate the critical difference between the two methods, imagine two successive coin tosses. According to theorist Justin Joque, "[frequentism] defines probability as the long-run frequency of a system."[8] A frequentist analysis of two tossed coins would entail a one-in-four chance that both coins would land on tails. If the first coin was tossed and happened to land on its tail, the likelihood of the two coins both landing on tails would remain one in four. Rather than stable predictions of entire systems, Bayes's Method allows predictions to be updated after each discrete event. A Bayesian analysis would begin with the same one-in-four odds, but after the first coin landed on its tail, the odds would be recalculated and improved to one-in-two. While frequentism either confirms or refutes a stable hypothesis, Bayesian methods reformulate hypotheses after each measurable event.

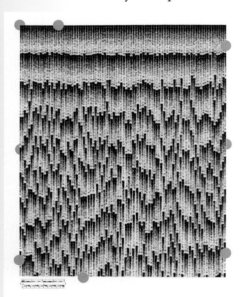

⋏ Print produced with a CNC inkjet printer registering the unique digital profiles of 48 anonymous online workers. Curtis Roth, *Drawing 2.1* (2019).

Unlike frequentism, Bayesian methods don't require a truth to confirm or refute. Instead, they calculate operative truths in real time. Applying a Bayesian analysis to a thousand flipped coins rather than just two would mean that one's initial hypothesis about the outcome could be entirely arbitrary. As long as one possessed the computational power to tune their hypothesis after each successive flip, they wouldn't even need to start with the knowledge that a coin had a second side at all. While frequentism might confirm or refute reasonable correlations like those between exercise and romance, Bayesian methods fabricate previously unimaginable worlds, like one in which a user's sex life can be correlated with their transportation patterns.

8 Justin Joque, "Chances Are," *Real-Life Magazine*, March 28, 2019.

For many, the agnosticism of Bayesian methods suggests the growing obsolescence of theory itself. According to British entrepreneur Chris Anderson, "Who knows why people do what they do? The point is they do it, and we can track and measure it with unprecedented fidelity. With enough data, the numbers speak for themselves."[9] Today numbers that speak for themselves underwrite virtually all contemporary machine learning processes. Their continual recalculations of actionable truths account for neural networks' enormous expenditure of energy.[10] If this isn't unnerving enough, Bayes's Method not only processes our possible futures, but is increasingly regarded, in certain circles, as a quasi-morality for re-designing our own cognition.

MIND DESIGN

LessWrong is a techno-utopian self-care community founded by Singularity Institute researcher Eliezer Yudkowsky. It began in 2009, following a series of blog posts by Yudkowsky on the benefits of applying Bayesian methods to his own cognitive processes in order to achieve higher states of self-fulfillment.[11] Today, LessWrong's nearly 10,000 members predominantly congregate in an online discussion forum devoted to rationality training. The organization's more dedicated members participate in popular offline meetings and co-living arrangements in New York, San Francisco, and a handful of other metropolitan areas. The in-person meetings involve everything from board games and thought experiments to more intense experiences involving psychedelics, swinging, and rationalist group therapy.

At the core of LessWrong's commitment to rationality lies the aphoristic invocation of Bayes's statistical methods. An influential article by long-time LessWrong member Kaj Sotala defines the group's application of Bayesianism through three core tenets:

1. Any given observation has many different possible causes.
2. How we interpret *any* event, and the new information we get from anything, depends on information we *already* had.
3. We can use the concept of probability to measure our subjective

9 Chris Anderson, "The End of Theory," *Wired*, June 23, 2008.
10 Will Knight, "AI Can Do Great Things – If It Doesn't Burn the Planet," *Wired*, January 23, 2020.
11 Nitasha Tiku, "Faith, Hope and Singularity: Entering the Matrix with New York's Futurist Set," *Observer*, July 25, 2012.
12 Kaj Sotala, "What is Bayesianism?," *LessWrong*, February 26, 2010, https://www.lesswrong.com/posts/AN2cBr6xKWCB8dRQG/what-is-bayesianism.

belief in something. Furthermore, we can apply the mathematical laws regarding probability to choosing between different beliefs. If we want our beliefs to be correct, we *must* do so.[12]

From Sotala's tenets, one could assume LessWrong offers little more than basically good advice. Thinking critically about the world, considering your own biases, and working to overcome your erroneous beliefs are obvious but helpful things for anyone to remember. These core tenets guide group members in everything from developing strategies for avoiding workplace conflicts to playing out elaborate techno-utopian futures through discussion board hypotheticals entailing mobile mega-cities and malevolent artificial intelligence. But the generalist sensibility of LessWrong's approach to rational mindfulness begs the question, why invoke Bayes's theories at all?

In practice, LessWrong's members rely on Bayesianism less as a technical theory of probability than a spiritual proverb repeated in the hopes of discovering a higher rationality. Group member and popular YouTube rationality coach Julia Galef claims, "It's not like I go around plugging numbers into this formula all day; it's more like, having my brain steeped in Bayes has qualitatively changed the way that I think on a daily basis."[13] While Galef refers to the process as steeping, Yudkowsky himself has described the use of soft-Bayesian meditation as "mind design." For Yudkowsky, designing one's mind requires visualizing your brain from the outside.[14] Like other self-help movements emerging from Silicon Valley (e.g., Neuro-Linguistic Programming [NLP] or Quantified Self [QS]), Yudkowsky and his fellow LessWrong members achieve the objective removal of a designer by reframing their

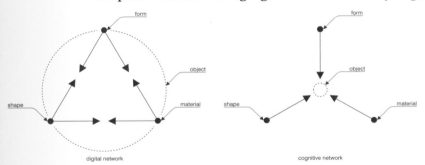

⋀ A description of the differences between conventional digital networks and human cognitive networks, after Eliezer Yudkowsky's "Disguised Queries."[15] Courtesy of Curtis Roth.

13 Julia Galef, "Bayes: How one equation changed the way I think," *YouTube*, June 3, 2013, https://www.youtube.com/watch?v=za7RqnT7CMo&feature=emb_title.

14 Eliezer Yudkowsky, "How An Algorithm Feels From The Inside," *LessWrong*, February 10, 2008, https://www.lesswrong.com/posts/yA4gF5KrboK2m2Xu7/how-an-algorithm-feels-from-inside.

15 See Eliezer Yudkowsky, "Disguised Queries," *LessWrong*, February 8, 2008, https://www.lesswrong.com/posts/4FcxgdvdQP45D6Skg/disguised-queries.

own intellection as a computational process. Through a host of digital metaphors that have become common parlance amongst the group, Yudkowsky refers to mindsets as "self-designed neural networks," and insists that intuition is simply "feeling an algorithm from the inside." For LessWrong, Bayesianism isn't a statistical practice so much as a mantra, and like any good mantra, when repeated enough, Bayesianism holds the power to shift its disciple's attention from the interior of their own algorithms to an outside where the mind (like any other piece of software) might be designed.

While the majority of LessWrong's members apply the strategies of mind-design in order to better manage the volatility of their own lives, Yudkowsky's future ends somewhere far stranger. Through his work with the Peter Thiel–funded Singularity Institute, Yudkowsky argues for a reconsideration of human intelligence as planet earth's most valuable resource.[16] According to Yudkowsky, if all technology is the product of intelligence then, like cultivating soil, disciplining our intelligence will inevitably accelerate humanity's technological progress.[17] The messianic implications of Yudkowsky's

mind-design anticipate forms of artificial super-intelligence capable of closing the singularity loop in the form of digital systems so smart they can engineer their own advancement. All human cognition—if properly designed—is thus nothing more than a present-day simulation of a future digital singularity.

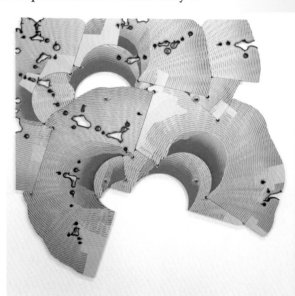

Yudkowsky's understanding of "design" isn't ultimately that different from the term's more commonplace uses, long-premised on a mediated remove between the designer and the object(s) of their design. In the case of architectural design, this remove comes in the form of an architect's various instruments of production. For Yudkowsky however, the mind

➤ Painting produced with a custom CNC device painting the recorded wrist movements of 21 anonymous online workers. Curtis Roth, *Wrist Painting 3* (2019).

16 Bryan Gardiner, "Peter Thiel Explains How to Invest in the Singularity," *Wired*, September 9, 2007, https://www.wired.com/2007/09/peter-thiel-exp/.
17 Eliezer Yudkowsky, "Five Minute Singularity Intro," 2007, https://yudkowsky.net/singularity/intro/.

is at once a design instrument, the object of design, and the designer themselves. Paired with an understanding of life as merely manageable flows of information independent of their bodily substrates, the mind becomes a plastic medium enough like a computer to serve as a scale-model of computation to come. But if LessWrong imagines mind design as a pseudo-religious commitment to cleansing oneself from irrationality, much of the current investment in Bayesian artificial intelligence isn't oriented toward achieving higher orders of rationality, but toward approximating precisely the protean tendencies that Yudkowsky and his disciples hope to purge from their minds.[18]

PROTEAN CAPTURE

As an example, we could look to the increasingly sophisticated neural networks that underpin ongoing efforts to realize self-driving vehicles. These networks guide the car's decision-making processes by interpreting the information received from an array of body-mounted cameras, radar, and LIDAR sensors. While the architecture of these neural networks are proprietary, each relies on a process called "semantic segmentation," or the interpretive method in which arrays of pixels and sensor information are assigned the values of semantic objects such as pedestrians, sidewalks, and other vehicles. While acting on specific semantic interpretations by steering, accelerating, or braking depends on comparatively easy if/then logic structures, today our self-driving future depends on replicating the productively irrational ways in which human drivers interpret sensory information.

AI systems like self-driving vehicles are often dystopically described as replacing humans by emulating cognitive processes like visual discernment, but, more accurately, segmentation should be understood as a way to parcel sensor data and the mind itself into discrete units that are more capable of being outsourced and captured. In order for a computer to see, thousands of human beings first need to demonstrate seeing hundreds of thousands of times. Semantic segmentation algorithms rely on vast libraries of sample images that have been pre-segmented by mostly anonymous online workers.

18 My use of the term "protean" in this text is informed by evolutionary researcher Geoffrey F. Miller's analysis of proteanism in primates. Miller has theorized the evolution of seemingly chaotic behaviors as both a defensive strategy against so-called Machiavellian Intelligence, and as a potential causal explanation for human creativity. See Geoffrey Miller. "Protean Primates: The Evolution of Adaptive Unpredictability in Competition and Courtship" in *Machiavellian Intelligence II*, ed. Andrew Whiten & Richard Byrne (Cambridge: Cambridge University Press, 1997).
19 In 2017, Amazon introduced Amazon SageMaker, a cloud-based machine-learning platform designed to integrate with Amazon's online micro-labor platform Mechanical Turk.

These geographically dispersed laborers segment pre-selected images by outlining apparent objects.[19] Once hundreds of thousands of pedestrians, trees, or curbs have been manually identified by human workers, a neural network filtering sensor information through Bayesian statistical methods can effectively determine a particular pixel field's correspondence to a specific semantic object from a catalog of possibilities. When a self-driving vehicle swerves to avoid a pedestrian, the labor of thousands of disparate workers is mobilized to guide the car toward a statistically preferable outcome.

While self-actualization practices like Yudkowsky's treat the mind as a paper space for modeling a computation to come, semantic segmentation economies prioritize a different understanding of the mind altogether—one in which life is the confluence of infinitely divisible components, each capable of being captured and managed from a distance.[20] For example, a self-driving car can be more efficiently trained by disentangling an anonymous online worker's visual faculties from their emotional need to find fulfillment in their work or a meaningful community with their colleagues. This divisible economy of the mind treats cognition as a catalog of possible software extensions.[21] These extensions mine our protean natures so as to supply artificial intelligence systems with faculties like creativity or capriciousness that remain impossible to engineer digitally. Seen in this light, self-driving vehicles don't replace drivers, they displace drivers into the dividuated software extensions of onboard algorithms.

A DOLLY PARTON DIGITAL POLITICS

Whether the mind is a model of a computer to come or an extension of the computers we already have, Bayes's Method has facilitated an age defined by the techno-social project of "anthropoforming."[22] Until recently, the long arch of the Anthropocene has been primarily defined by terraforming practices—or the modification of the earth and its environments in order to render it more amenable to human life.[23] Today, anthropoforming is terraforming's strange inversion: the remodeling of life itself in order to lubricate its interface with global computational

---

20 For a more detailed description of dividuation, see: Gilles Deleuze, "Postscript on the Societies of Control," *October*, Vol. 59, Winter, 1992.

21 Sebastian Schmieg, "Humans as Software Extensions, Will You Be My Plugin?," Filmed December 28, 2017 at #34c3, Leipzig, Germany. https://media.ccc.de/v/34c3-9077-humans_as_software_extensions.

22 Helen Hester, "TTF 2020 – Keynote," Filmed July 7, 2020. https://www.youtube.com/watch?v=Y-1fnG9iA5RA.

23 With terraforming, I am referring to an almost uselessly broad range of human practices including architecture, agriculture, economics, and most forms of engineering, among others.

networks. Anthropoforming practices design life by treating it both as a sandbox for computational innovation and a raw material resource for outsourcing faculties that are difficult to simulate digitally.

While Parton's meme stopped at four squares, living in the age of anthropoforming means that each of us has already been parceled into thousands of disparate selves. These fragments of ourselves now labor within innumerable predictive processes, from Google's ad-targeting algorithms to the CIA's real-time citizenship modeling.[24] In this context, Bayesianism acts as the conceptual apparatus that makes anthropoforming both possible and inevitable. The Bayesian method provides the predictive framework through which raw behavioral data is interpreted, and the perpetually deferred nature of any Bayesian prediction means that every interpreted behavior merely refines the criteria for future behavioral capture. While AI theorists like Yudkowsky anticipate an approaching singularity in which a computer will eventually engineer its own advancement, the always-appended worldview of today's Bayesian processes *already* entail thousands of soft-singularities.

The relentless divisions imposed by anthropoforming practices are evident in our fixation on fulfillment as the most compelling avenue of political resistance. Through recent initiatives like the European Union's General Data Protection Regulation (GDPR) or net neutrality activism in the United States, today's politics of fulfillment promise to reconsolidate a unified self through appeals to the individual's historical rights of privacy and cognitive autonomy. While such appeals might be useful stopgaps in the short term, they also reify a possessive individualism that regards the ownership of one's autonomy as a precondition to a market economy organized around the ownership of resources.[25] Fulfillment in this context is the legal right to opt-out, to toggle our privacy settings or perhaps even to be forgotten. But as theorist Katrina Forrester has recently pointed out, "[such measures] rarely try to disperse the ownership of our data— by breaking the power monopolies that collect it, or by placing its use under democratic control through public oversight."[26] Instead of consolidating ourselves around ideals of fulfillment, what if we were

24 John Cheney-Lippold, *We Are Data, Algorithms and the Making of our Digital Selves*, New York University Press, 2017.
25 C. B. Macpherson, *The Political Theory of Possessive Individualism: Hobbes to Locke*, Oxford University Press, 1962. On the relationship between the fulfilled individual and the market economy, Macpherson argues, "Its possessive quality is found in its conception of the individual as essentially the proprietor of his own person or capacities, owing nothing to society for them ... The human essence is freedom from the wills of others, and freedom is a function of possession."
26 Katrina Forrester, "Known Unknowns," *Harper's*, September 2018.

to imagine a politics modeled after Parton's "woman who can do it all." A democracy for an age of anthropoforming. One in which our power wasn't consolidated around aging ideals of individual autonomy or personal fulfillment, but precisely in our relentless multiplication.

What makes Bayes's method so powerful is its ability to calculate the influence of specific inputs in the determination of a particular prediction, whether those inputs are individual coin flips, Uber rides, or segmented curbs. Today these inputs are fragments of our protean selves, our captured creativity, generated by our labor, and mined through our interactions online. But they are also almost exclusively owned and managed by corporate proprietors. Whenever Google Ads successfully predicts an ad click-through, the updated algorithm contains a precise leger documenting how that prediction was made and the weight that each of our divided selves contributed toward calculating that prediction. A politics after Dolly Parton would entail seeing these mined behaviors not merely as our alienated labor, but as our divided selves residing elsewhere. It would require models of subjectivity that undo the outdated distinction between users and the information their lives generate. And most importantly, it would refuse fulfillment in favor of a political power that depends on our fragmentation.

While this all seems only about as likely as LessWrong's walking megacities, perhaps a place to begin is endeavoring to produce work that allows us to exist more than once. Work like Dolly Parton's four-square meme, defined by our being multiplied through so many digital interfaces. A kind of work that would speculate on the ways in which such multiplications afford new kinds of communities and new ways to care for one another. While this may be modest compared to the increasingly intimate capturing of our lives by contemporary digital capitalists, perhaps it would be a meaningful way to begin demanding agency over the technologies that are fabricated from, and act upon, our multiplied lives.

POSTCOMMODITY STRATEGIES FOR POSTCOMMODITY TIMES: AN EVOLVING TOOLKIT
Laida Aguirre

Λ stock-a-studio, *Stock Catalog* (2015–2020). Courtesy of Laida Aguirre.

Intro: Contextualize Terms: POSTCOMMODITY/POSTCOMMODITIES

A. Introduce
— Spam in your inbox, junk in your mailbox, pay for storage, TMI, full thumb drive … all the drawers are full yet there are items in the cart. We are in a moment of material reckoning. The current production model of *more, faster, cheaper* has created a counterproductive muchness, a saturation of commodities accelerated by a tightening culture-commodity loop that determines what is culture today, product tomorrow, trash the next. From extraction practices to distribution centers to material catalogs, architecture is implicated in all scales of this saturation. If making objects and material environments has consequences, we are in a time of increasing consequences.
— Postcommodity calls out a contradictory condition. As excess relies on scarcity and produces more of both.
— Commodities are sociomaterial objects: they combine practical and economic factors such as availability and affordability with highly subjective ones like trends and color preferences, making it necessary for this toolset to address both logistical and aesthetic factors.
— Design directly reflects these sociomaterial circumstances, these material entanglements that link a "new downstairs bathroom" Pinterest folder directly to sales of tiles and what is considered "cute" on social media to material extraction demands in a quarry halfway around the world.
— To design in sync with the now-times is to design through postcommodity.
— Postcommodity marks a post-convenience material context, a condition where one designs with recirculation in mind, where not much is new and all can be renewed.
— Work during postcommodity begins from that abundance, from that excess—the muchness we have produced—and attempts to instill new life from and onto it.
— Looking at what is already around us, the latent oddities and mundane nature of the products, materials, and resources, the stuff that we have chosen to make, we must ask ourselves how it becomes product, what are the economies or frameworks that make these things move around and exchange hands, and who gets access to these resources?
— A design process where the material life cycle of the project is an early consideration; design rarely begins from raw materials but rather from the stuff we have already made, the muchness all around us. Repurposing, reassembling, reimagining, recirculating to new ends, these are the design strategies of the postcommodity times.

B. Explain
— Postcommodities are opportunistic, responding to existing conditions; they foreground a designer's ability to extract possibilities and value from within the limitations of existing matter.
— Postcommodities are interested in inverting the conventional loop, using the commodity to platform culture rather than using culture to promote commodity.
— They are in an endless loop of use, maintenance, and reimagination. They create additional loops within these existing economic loops.
— Postcommodities are perpetually in flux as objects with continuously expanding life cycles; shifting appearance here becomes a form of mobility.
— In this postcommodity condition, effort and material knowledge replace convenience … dealing with already-made objects and used materials replaces a baseline of existing standards with material idiosyncrasy. Not much begins with clean 4x8 sheets and clean untreated surfaces but instead must begin from an assessment of material conditions and possibilities left over within objects after they fulfill their initial use. By adding steps to the

beginning and end, this process in turn defines the design process and its outcomes.
— Since it does not begin from standards, it is more work.
— Postcommodity tends to understand the material world through multipliers where a thing x many OR a thing x often OR a thing x everywhere can be a resource (can also be architecture).
— It argues that the material-geopolitical can also be found in a single bolt.

C. Tools
— Postcommodity has a tactical design toolkit that helps commodities become resources and stay in constant transition, allowing them to re-enter a material loop over and over again. These are processes, logistics, and methodologies for designers to work within idiosyncratic, more complex material spaces. They engage questions of aesthetics and material life-cycle logics, entangling technicality and material savviness with cultural and logistical factors.
— The toolkit combines intimate material knowledge—such as finishes and product compatibilities—with knowledge of the extra-material factors and networks that qualify, proliferate, and create desires around them. They renew desire for existing objects rather than create desire for new ones.
  ★ Examples of material strategies: stickers, posters, paint, wallpaper, cover swaps, taking off layers, patching, flipping inside out, cleaning, reupholstering, alterations, renewing surface, jerry rigging, etc.
  ★ Examples of extra-material factors: maintenance, care, material knowledge, design thinking, labor, networks of acquisition/redistribution, etc.

D. Ethos of POSTCOMMODITY/POSTCOMMODITIES

POSTCOMMODITY CONCEPT:	REPLACES:	STRATEGY:	DIGITAL AID:	TO STUDY:
Freshness	Newness	Layers	Subjectivity: image overlay + refresh	Wallpapers/posters
Aggregated	Singularity	Modularity	Iterations/repetition	Milk crates
Material integrity	Complex shapes	Whole cuts	Cut sheet planning	Off cuts
Error = opportunity	Error = waste	Material Toolkit	Inventory of ideas	Freecycle
Parts	Wholeness	Disassemblage	Future reconfiguration	DfD*/event architecture
Care	Landfill	Maintenance	Housework/DIY knowledge videos	Preservation techniques

DfD: Design for Disassembly

E. Stock examples
— Attempts to respond to the availability of stuff while refusing singular ruling paradigms: i.e., to maintain aesthetic diversity and pluralism that does not lead to excess waste, we must think through and evolve the postcommodity toolkit to put together future-aware material strategies while allowing for variation.
— Generally functioning within a small margin between the singular and the plural; the complex and the generic; the off-the-shelf and the authored; and the aesthetic and the pragmatic.
— Below are three examples of postcommodity projects from 2015–2020. They illustrate three techniques that work toward postcommodity:
  ★ RETURN: Design for *reimbursement*
  ★ RESURFACE: Design for *keeping*
  ★ RECIRCULATE: Design for *reassembly*

Body: Illustrate Term: POSTCOMMODITY/POSTCOMMODITIES
1. RETURN
A. Main:
— Design for *reimbursement*
— Takes advantage of big-box point-of-sale contracts
— Main tactics:

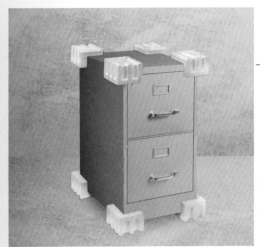

▲ Protecting returns. stock-a-studio.
Courtesy of Laida Aguirre.

* Accounting: keep receipts
* Care: keep packaging and do not damage goods

B. Related scholarship
— Easterling's "Subtraction"
* Keller Easterling's book "Subtraction" asks architects to consider the possibilities of designing with intention for a building's eventual removal. While design for subtraction, or building removal, offers more opportunity for design, it also provides an economy that "must also deploy active forms … time-released protocols that generate or manage these exchanges with a stream of objects and spaces." Subtraction is "a heavy industry, a source of employment, a material resource, a global environmental protocol, and an alternative market that escapes the dominance of the financial industry."[1]
* Easterling asserts that the subtraction economy "almost exists," noting that the "creative trick lies in designing its political disposition—the spin that gives the idea enough traction and scale to interrupt free-market doom loops or other political stalemates."[2]
* As global e-commerce exacerbates overconsumption by way of convenience, designing through the return policy can be an effective method to enact Easterling's provocation.

C. Work example: STOCK INSTAGRAM
— 2015–2020, Instagram
— Project: Construction product representation project that uses Instagram to create an alternative and speculative material catalog.
— Concerned with access to material resources, the project takes advantage of big-box store return policies to create over 600 images by purchasing, staging, photographing, and returning construction materials on a $200 credit.
— Reauthors off-the-shelf materials to create a new catalog.
— Examines the ways we can reframe products and readymades as future-minded design elements that can compel new subjectivities, and with them, new forms of world-making and representation while shedding the ownership tendencies associated with commodities.
— A scrappy, resource-limited approach to architectural projects that tries to take advantage of a commercial loophole.
— Deploys conventional commercial gimmicks like fetishizing objects through portraiture, studio lighting, and calculated backdrops, yet creates no added commercial value.
— This project did not affect the sale of cinder blocks or flexible PVC plumbing elbows in any given month. What STOCK really proposed was a method of producing a lot from very little, often proposing entire worlds using a single material texture or image.
— Engages not only the spatial products of architecture but the material economies within which they exist and rendered explicit the often-silent

1 Keller Easterling, *Subtraction*, Critical Spatial Practice 4 (Sternberg Press, 2014).
2 Ibid.

economies of architectural projects, big and small.
— Allows for the production of an extensive body of work while side-stepping many of the usual flaws of the temporary architectural project: waste, lack of sufficient funding, storage fees, etc., while, admittedly, exchanging those for my own labor.

2. RESURFACE
A. Main
— Design for *keeping*
— Spatial commodity resurfacing services that refresh architectures and furniture by simply changing the surfaces in order to renew or widen their appeal and keep them from being discarded.
— Intends to re-appeal to our aesthetic desires by changing the surfaces of our existing commodities as a way to lessen waste.
— Responds to the closed loop of influence between material and culture: to make it cool again is to renew our desires to keep things we already own.
— Main assumption: We don't throw away things that we continue to like.
— Main tactics:
  * Renew surface while maintaining material core intact
  * Requires fine-grain material knowledge such as adhesiveness, elasticity, product interaction specifications.

⋀ Furniture resurfacing. stock-a-studio. Courtesy of Laida Aguirre.

B. Related scholarship
— Sianne Ngai's *Our Aesthetic Categories: Zany, Cute, Interesting*
  * In her book, Ngai lays out that the *cute* has to do with consumption, particularly with how we construct relationships with the objects we consume. The *zany*, she argues, has to do with production, and more specifically with the sorts of performance involved with contemporary labor. The *interesting*, finally, has to do with circulation, and draws attention to the relentless streams of information associated with advanced capitalism.[3]
— Iñaki Ábalos's "Warhol at the Factory"
  * From 1962–1984, an industrial space turned social hub whose interior was fully wrapped in rugged tin foil became the creative pulse of the Beat generation. Otherwise known as Warhol's "Factory," the uncommon decor gave the otherwise "more neutral industrial space a progressive and contestatory charisma, a seductiveness" as well as an air of avant-gardism, which gave the space an identity as an urban commune but would later be commercialized into the notion of the "NY loft artist" space. In "Warhol at The Factory: from Freudo-marxist communes to the New York loft", Iñaki Ábalos understands this as the

3 Sianne Ngai, *Our Aesthetic Categories: Zany, Cute, Interesting* (Harvard University Press, 2015).
4 Iñaki Ábalos, "Warhol at The Factory: From Freudo-marxist communes to the New York loft," *The Good Life: A Guided Visit to the Houses of Modernity* (Park Books, 2017).

eventual commercialization of the urban commune through the instrumentalization of the socio-political aesthetics of the factory's radical decor.[4]

★ The factory here serves as an example of the relationship between decor and value within a real estate context, a relationship that has been optimized most obviously by companies like AirBNB and WeLive, who have developed decor algorithms that automate and optimize the furniture, materials, and finishes of apartments in order to appeal to select clientele. *Hardcore-Redecore* proposes to use the unique off-market position of a case study house, as a property that is not seeking additional commercial value but rather attempts to perform as a cultural hub, to carry out a series of public mixed-reality redecoration sessions that unlink decor from profit margins and aesthetics from marketable hype.

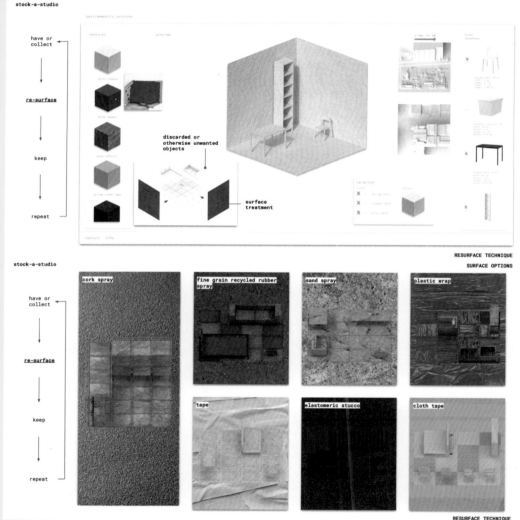

Resurfacing technique and options. stock-a-studio, *HARDCORE.REDECORE* (2021 work in progress). Courtesy of Laida Aguirre.

C. Work example: HARDCORE-REDECORE
— 2021, Work in Progress
— *Hardcore-Redecore* is a spatial commodity resurfacing service that invites the public to participate in a speculative design process to resurface a modernist case study house using currently available inventories of materials and aesthetic preferences.
— Through materials that are cheap, or easy to produce, *Hardcore-Redecore* updates the case study house to a current material and aesthetic context.
— By opening up the case study house to a multi-author framework, a static preservation project goes through a public and contextualized transformation.
— Attempts to invigorate the public's interest by putting that which is static and has a fixed narrative back into circulation by renegotiating its public appeal.
— Material strategies include: spraying, wallpapering, painting, dipping, wrapping, taping, etc.
— The project translates publicly sourced proposals by visualizing them through a digital interactive three-dimensional environment complemented with a series of material mock-ups and material samples.
— The audience will be able to walk through an interactive three-dimensional digitally redone VDL house as well as see material samples associated with each proposal.
— The goal of the project is to create a mixed material-digital project that ushers in a reimagination of the VDL through new speculative material contexts.
— Giving the house a public aesthetic availability and creating an aesthetic loop between architect and audience.

3. RECIRCULATE
A. Main
— Design for *disassembly/reassembly*
— Main tactic: Material kits. Assemble material parts using non-invasive

⋀ Basics with logos. stock-a-studio. Courtesy of Laida Aguirre.

⋀ Event tent. stock-a-studio. Courtesy of Laida Aguirre.

assemblage systems: bolts not screws.
— Main assumption: Things are less wasteful when they remain useful. Things are less wasteful when they can adapt to changes.
— Parts come together to form a packable, shippable, and easy-to-assemble kit that can adapt to different sites and activities.
— Usually involves assembling off-the-shelf products.
    ⋆ If cutting materials, maintain self-similar and whole size cuts. Easier to hand over to new users.
B. Related scholarship
— Peggy Deamer's "Detail Deliberations"
    ⋆ Although the text addresses parametricism rather than design for disassembly, Deamer advises us to "Dispense with fixed identities all together," challenging architects to design with consideration for aspects of the systems within which it exists.
    ⋆ "But at the scale of the detail, the manner in which assembly, usually at the backend of design, is brought to the front has significant repercussions."
    ⋆ She argues that the temporal and logistical collapse of parametricism's information density rearranged the modernist hierarchy of design and assembly, as "labor and material information regarding assembly at the back end informs design at the front end."[5]
C. Work example I: [A KIT OF THESE SOME PARTS] X BUDGET GYM]

— 2018, Materials & Applications storefront, Los Angeles
— Project: A public gym, material prototype, video game prototype, and public programming
— Temporary architectural assembly of digital and physical materials in service of an activity: in this case, working out.
— Demo kit for deployable and customizable kit of parts that can be assembled together to form temporary architecture or furniture.
— The kit includes: a powder-coated structural steel system, foam padding, water weights (or ballasts), tape, tarp (shade or privacy), ratchet straps (structural tie), shims (foundation adjustment), inflatable dunnage bags (furniture and padding), sandbags (counterweights), and printed/vacuum-formed panels (shade and privacy).

↗ stock-a-studio, [a kit of these some parts] x budget gym] (2018). Courtesy of Laida Aguirre.

— An architectural microcosm: strapped together and padded up, easily taken apart to be passed on to the next user.
— The space serves as a space for working out, a hydration station for pre-designed local hikes/bike routes, and a platform to showcase local artists who have body-related practices.
— Co-opts architectural formulas of mobile architectures such as concert rigs, rentable event tents, or information booths,

5 Peggy Deamer, "Detail Deliberations," in Building (in) the Future: Recasting Labor in Architecture (Princeton Architectural Press, 2012), 80–90.

where often durable structural frames are combined with low-budget material assemblies that are re-aestheticized and reassembled to serve future events while also needing to be flatpacked for transport.

— Part standard, part custom, it combines the scenographic with the utilitarian.

— Intertwines custom with generic elements and images with budget materials to provide a set of parts that forms a gym initially and a prototype for other programs later on.

— Reuses the same materials over and over, reprinting and repainting on top of the last print: it becomes both an accessible approach to aesthetic renewal and a proposal for more future-minded construction/assemblage tactics.

— Resting on the straightforwardness of its base structure, the kit focuses its design agency in developing non-invasive attachments that allow for the dismantling and redistribution of the parts that make it able to serve future uses.

— Proposes assembly, not construction, using rather than owning, refinishing rather than repurchasing as ways of creating an architectural kit with equal consideration of aesthetics and its own future reuse.

— The project includes a website where people can customize select parts in order to adapt it to their needs as a traveling scenography.

— The project also includes a video game where one can pick and change the parts of the kit creating an embodied catalog.

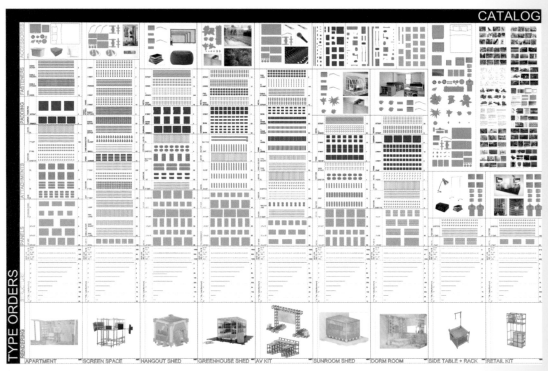

Total inventory/every part accounted. stock-a-studio. Courtesy of Laida Aguirre.

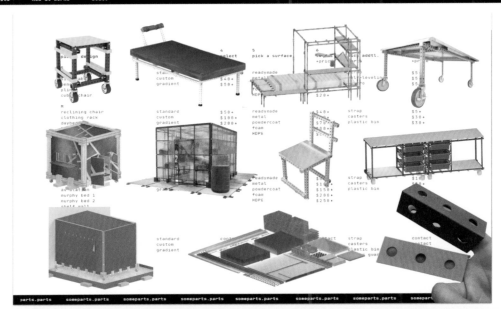

Catalog. stock-a-studio, [*someparts.parts*] (2019). Courtesy of Laida Aguirre.

B. Work example II: [SOMEPARTS.PARTS]
— 2019: ongoing, internet, everywhere USPS ships
— Project: Web-based catalog of small architectures/furniture kits.
— Pivots the same structural system as above toward a general audience, less venues and institutions.
— Perpetually useful, multi-scalar, flat-packed modular small architectures/furniture kit.
— A response to fast-furniture, which is often single-use/throwaway furniture due to its poor construction and cheap materiality.
— Fast furniture is one of the largest contributors to these damaging material life cycles. Each year, according to the EPA, in the US alone 12 million tons of furniture and furnishings are trashed. Only a small percentage is recycled. Fast furniture is right behind fast fashion as one of the top environmental fiascos.[6]
— Someparts.parts is durable and reconfigurable. As the user's needs evolve, the kit can evolve, too.
— The kit attempts to acknowledge the full life cycle of these objects by making them disassemblable and returnable to the seller. It is never to be thrown away.
— Each kit comes with instructions on how to assemble as well as alternative designs that the kit can create.

6 Simon Usborne, "Silly Billy: what the Ikea bookcase tells us about the true cost of fast furniture," *The Guardian*, May 19, 2020, https://www.theguardian.com/lifeandstyle/2020/may/19/silly-billy-what-the-ikea-bookcase-tells-us-about-the-true-cost-of-fast-furniture.

— Common parts: Aluminum square tubing + stain resistant surfaces + ⅛″ aluminum sheet
— Relies on:
  ∗ Self-assembly, no special tools or knowledge needed.
  ∗ Non-invasive assembly methods: nuts and bolts and ratchet straps. Makes parts reusable as they are unaffected in the assembly process.
  ∗ Uses uncut, whole size sheet material. Makes parts reusable as they are kept at useful dimensions.
  ∗ Standard size is key as users can perform size-based material searches and all results can be applied to the kit. Any 1'x1' or 2'x2' piece of material can become a surface or a seat or a shelf.

Conclusion: Additional Outcomes of POSTCOMMODITY/POSTCOMMODITIES
A. Evolving thoughts
Postcommodity
— Is designing between materials and their consequences.
— Expands the timeline of a project to include before/after use through material life-cycle considerations.
— Creates additional loops within existing material and economic loops.
— Uses commodities to platform culture rather than culture to promote commodities.
— Produces new modes of engagement between public and architect, through input-based design process that includes options and variables.
— Creates hybrid digital + physical, image + material, tectonic + logistical strategies and environments.
— Foregrounds scenographic approach, aesthetic flexibilities, and resource accessibilities.
— Is material after materialism: a post-stuff design thinking.

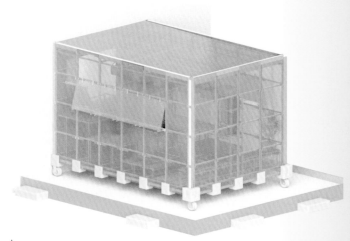

⋏ Someparts_sunroom. stock-a-studio, [someparts.parts] (2019). Courtesy of Laida Aguirre.

MATERIAL
FULFILLMENT

BUILDING WITH AIR
Ang Li

➤ Site-specific installation for *Space p11* in the Chicago Pedway that consisted of nine eight-foot columns constructed out of discarded EPS foam, each mounted on recessed casters that visitors could move around the narrow confines of the gallery. Ang Li, *All That Is Solid* (2019). Photo: Nathan Keay.

A series of monolithic columns filled an empty storefront gallery in the Chicago Pedway, spanning the full height of the room.[1] The objects were uniform in shape and color, each displaying an aggregate, rock-like texture that recalled older forms of masonry construction at odds with the architecture of the concourse. Upon closer inspection, they revealed an irregular patchwork of familiar profiles that harkened back to a more recent archaeology—electronics packaging, food containers, disposable coolers, etc. Each column was composed out of roughly 50 cubic feet of expanded polystyrene foam, or EPS foam, collected from recycling centers in the Greater Chicago area, cleaned and tightly shrink-wrapped into nine columns, measuring eight feet in height. This collection of fragments passed through many other stops before finding its way here, including assembly lines, retail warehouses, distribution centers, domestic living rooms, empty garages, storage units, and recycling facilities, not to mention the countless trucks and shipping containers that transported them between these far-flung sites of production and consumption. The collective effort that it took to bring them here, to be put on display in the contained space of a gallery suggests that they are of some value. But what kind of value? Are we to read them as trash, or commodity? As raw material, or art objects? Have they been placed here in order to fill an otherwise empty room quickly and cheaply? Or do they speak to a deeper and more conflicted search for material fulfillment that lies at the very heart of contemporary architectural production?

Twentieth-century accounts of architectural materiality were often predicated on human-centric notions of material "honesty" and "integrity," in which architects are cast as humble interlocutors with the unique ability to give voice or shape to mute materials. Louis Kahn famously staged an imaginary conversation with a brick, in which he asked his students to consider what a brick wanted to be: "You say to brick, 'What do you want, brick?' And brick says to you, 'I like an arch.'"[2] This charming

Ang Li, *All That Is Solid* (2019). Photo: Nathan Keay.

1 This essay reflects on a body of material research into EPS foam that took place around an exhibition titled *All That is Solid*, exhibited at Space p11 in Chicago in September 2019, as a partner program to the 2019 Chicago Architecture Biennial. The project also builds on fieldwork conducted during a six-week residency at RAIR, a residency program located in a construction and demolition waste recycling center in Northeast Philadelphia.
2 Wendy Lesser, *You Say to Brick: The Life of Louis Kahn* (New York: Farrar, Straus and Giroux, 2018).

exchange upheld the modernist conceit that materials possess hidden designs or desires that can only be expressed through human intervention. Read in another way, it raises a pair of reciprocal questions around the changing nature of human-material collaborations. How do materials fulfill our needs and agendas, and in turn, how do they themselves *feel* fulfilled?

Building experiments with EPS foam conducted during a six-week residency at a construction and demolition waste recycling center in Northeast Philadelphia. Ang Li, *Balancing Acts* (2019). Photo: Billy Dufala.

To ask a brick what it wants to be seems willfully naïve today, when contemporary discussions around material agency are shaped by a wide web of external forces that extend beyond the boundaries and subjectivities of the building site. In a recent essay on the speech-carrying capacity of modern materials, architectural historian Mark Jarzombek offered an alternative framework for conversing with the material realm. Instead of asking materials what they want to be, he suggests, can we instead ask them what they have to say? As silent witnesses to repeating cycles of construction and destruction, building materials like steel, concrete, glass, and plastics hold clues to the contexts and conditions that lead to their production.[3] Instead of speaking on their behalf, through projection and ventriloquism, what kind of material truths would rise to the surface if these materials were allowed to speak for themselves?

EPS foam is a material that is shaped by its muteness. In a 1957 essay, Roland Barthes described the elusive appeal of petroleum-based products by describing them as a human-made enigma that "hardly exists as a substance." In his words, these synthetic materials are defined by their innate formlessness, "less a thing than the trace of a movement," whose infinite transformations "[give] man the measure of his own power."[4] His plastic mythology captured the indexical quality of materials like EPS foam and its ability to fulfill, through its very imma-

Ang Li, *Balancing Acts* (2019). Photo: Billy Dufala.

3 Mark Jarzombek, "The Quadrivium Industrial Complex," *e-flux* Journal, Overgrowth (November 2019), Accessed September 10, 2020, https://www.e-flux.com/architecture/overgrowth/296508/the-quadrivium-industrial-complex/.
4 Roland Barthes, "Plastic," *Mythologies* (New York, NY: Farrar, Straus and Giroux, 1991): 97–99.

teriality, the inflated desires of its makers and consumers. Designed to assume any size or shape, EPS foam has no stable expression of its own. Instead, it speaks through allusions, a physical register of shifting industry demands, production methods, and belief systems. As such, it is not so much a material that wants to be shaped, so much as one that asks to be read. The following essay attempts a series of close readings of this uniquely modern material in-situ—tracing it from its molecular origins to its global footprints—in order to examine what it has to say about architecture's inherited biases and hidden desires. These accounts trace the gradual procession of foam products through changing cultural attitudes, policy frameworks, and physical sites of production and consumption—from the factory floor, to the construction site, to the landfill. By placing these conflicting narratives of modern material fulfillment side by side, the piece unpacks the pliancy of EPS foam as well as its ability to challenge established cultural and aesthetic categories of product and byproduct, resource and refuse.

▲ Ang Li, *Balancing Acts* (2019). Photo: Billy Dufala.

WEIGHTLESSNESS

Composed of up to 98 percent air, EPS foam is a material that fulfills in the most literal sense. It was first developed by German chemists during World War II as an affordable substitute for balsa wood, an extremely lightweight timber product deployed for the construction of military aircrafts. As the first word in its name suggests, expanded polystyrene foam is a type of thermoplastic created through a chemical process in which raw beads of styrene—an organic compound derived from the petrochemical benzene—are heated by steam, causing them to expand into spherical pellets about 40 to 50 times their original volume. From there, the pellets are placed within molds and heated again to achieve a wide range of profiles and densities. This two-stage process enables very small amounts of raw styrene to be inflated, beyond recognition, to fill practically any desired volume.[5] The material efficiency of EPS foam echoed the culture of scarcity that defined the inter-war years.

▲ Ang Li, *Balancing Acts* (2019). Photo: Theo Mullen.

Like many other synthetic materials from the same period, its strength lay in its ability to mimic the physical and aesthetic properties of limited natural resources without any of their earthly entanglements. Beyond its practical applications, the thrill of having created something out of *almost* nothing imbued this human-made material with an aerial quality—matter conjured out of thin air.

Once it was unveiled to the post-war consumer market, EPS foam was rebranded as a "miracle material" that defied earthly constraints like weight, cost, and shelf life.[6] A promotional photograph from the Dow Chemical Company dating back to 1965 depicts a glamorous model in a bathing suit posing on top of a rectangular block of Styrofoam, adrift in "an unidentified body of water."[7] Another image from the same period portrays a young woman balancing an enormous log of foam effortlessly above her head. She is standing in front of a wall of identical foam logs, each cut to precisely the same length and diameter, arranged in stacks that recall the weightier stockpiles of a sawmill. Many similar images appear in the company's archives, featuring men, women, and sometimes children lifting blocks, logs, or sheets of this wondrous material with surprising ease. The humor and theatrics embedded in these demonstrations produce a kind of phenomenology of the immaterial that places them in the realm between science and spectacle. Through these images, the buoyant and lightweight properties of foam products were presented to the public as both an expanded material reality and a utopian

Model posed on log of Styrofoam adrift in a body of water, 1965. Photo: Dow Chemical Company Historical Image Collection. Courtesy of Science History Institute.

Model lifting a log of Dow Chemical Company Styrofoam over her head to demonstrate the product's buoyant and lightweight properties, 1949. Photo: Dow Chemical Company Historical Image Collection. Courtesy of Science History Institute.

5 Charles A. Breskin, "Expanding Fields for Expanded Plastics," *Scientific American*, Vol. 177, No. 3 (September 1947): 119–121.
6 Ibid.
7 Dow Chemical Company. "Model Posed on Log of Styrofoam," 1965. Dow Chemical Company Historical Image Collection, Box 4, Folder Products—Styrofoam. Science History Institute. Philadelphia. Quote taken from image caption.

vision of a future where weight and labor are rendered negligible by modern chemistry.

The illusion of weightlessness, evocatively captured in the Dow Chemical photographs, helped shape an increasingly dematerialized culture in which modern materials like EPS foam were promoted as artificial wonders with no origins and no consequences. The public perception of the chemical industry at the time reinforced the other-worldly connotations around expanded plastics, where manufacturers like Dow Chemical and DuPont were portrayed in the popular press as alchemists or "miracle workers" capable of fabricating just about anything out of "a lump of coal, a glass of water, and a whiff of atmosphere."[8] In their hands, the controlled space of the laboratory doubled as a site of chemical and cultural transformation, in which what was once natural became synthetic, and the image of plastics, as a proprietary consumer product, became increasingly divorced from its material reality.

INVISIBILITY

Within the built environment, EPS foam is defined in equal measure by its scalar potential and its ability to recede into the background—it is simultaneously everywhere and nowhere, abundant and invisible. As a highly effective space-filler, it is deployed in large quantities in both residential construction and large-scale infrastructure projects, where it doubles as a lightweight substitute for building mass. Yet its popularity relies on its discretion—it performs best when we are able to forget about its existence. Hidden between walls and beneath layers of topsoil, this universal placeholder makes up a substantial layer of the built environment that remains unseen—the invisible lining of modern society.

Designed to protect the comforts and conveniences we have come to associate with "modern living," foam insulation products continue to dominate the building industry as the most reliable form of separation between buildings and their surrounding environments. Valued for its ability to resist the effects of time and weather, this petroleum-based product has emerged as the unlikely symbol for green construction, the material of choice for meeting the performance requirements of passive homes and LEED standards.

8 Henry Smith Williams, "The Miracle-Worker: Modern Science in the Industrial World," *Everybody's* Magazine, 17 (October 1907): 498, quoted in Jeffrey Meikle, *American Plastic: A Cultural History* (New Brunswick, N.J: Rutgers University Press, 1995): 69.

The defensive properties of EPS foam are reinforced across scales, from the aerated molecular structure of the material itself, a cavity for trapping and storing heat, to the ways in which its insulating effects are standardized through building codes and performance metrics. Industry standards around foam products in the United States tend to focus on drawing correlations between the material's high thermal resistance—measured through its R-value—and its economic and environmental benefits—lower heating bills and energy footprints.[9] These figures work together to uphold a distinctly modernist view of environmental control, in which EPS foam serves as the literal and conceptual barrier between clearly defined binaries: interiors and exteriors, comfort and climate, human-made and natural.

Beyond the building envelope, foam's promise of monumentality without its consequences provided the material basis for unprecedented scales of human hubris. This drive toward bigger, faster, and longer-lasting structures at a fraction of the cost fed the development of new building products like EPS GeoFoam, a lightweight void fill developed in the 1970s for use on the construction of bridges, embankments, and landscaping projects.[10] With an average weight roughly 1 percent of the equivalent volume of soil, GeoFoam blocks were designed to fill large volumes of space without the typical costs associated with labor and transportation. In one striking example, a series of aerial photographs that documented the construction of the undulating land-

⋏   GeoFoam blocks during the construction of Maggie Daley Park, Chicago, 2013. Image: http://www.maggiedaleyparkcon struction.org

forms in Michael Van Valkenburgh's Maggie Daley Park in Chicago captured the frictionless appeal of this building block. In these images, nearly 20 acres of land above an existing parking garage were gradually covered from end to end by 75,000 cubic yards of GeoFoam blocks, each light enough to be maneuvered manually by no more

9 For further discussion on the relationship between R-values and the development of North American insulation theories, see Kiel Moe, "Insulating North America," *Construction History* 27 (2012): 87–106.
10 "Geofoam Takes a Walk in the Park," *Insulation Corporation of America*, April 29, 2014. Accessed September 10, 2020. https://insulationcorp.com/geofoam-takes-a-walk-in-the-park/.
11 Maggie Daley Park project page, *Walsh Construction* website. Accessed September 10, 2020. http://www.walshgroup.com/ourexperience/building/parksentertainment/maggiedaleypark.html.

than two or three workers.[11] Viewed through this lens, the messy material negotiations of an active job site were abstracted into an effortless composition that could be shaped and reshaped, quite literally, by human hands—an enormous massing model at 1:1 scale.

EXTERNALITIES

Reading EPS foam across scales, from its inflated molecular structure to the expansive building practices it has enabled leads to an inevitable set of questions: Does foam's ability to fulfill have a scalar limit? And if so, where does this build-up eventually end up? The illusion of weightlessness enables other forms of accumulation that unfold at the margins of our spatial imaginaries. At the domestic scale, this reveals itself in the familiar piles of packaging tucked away in our basements and garages. At the scale of the environment, foam's numerous disposable applications lead to a more persistent kind of backlog that is harder to ignore. EPS is notoriously difficult to recycle, a problem that can be traced back to its physical attributes. In a reuse industry where materials are priced by weight, the same airy quality that renders EPS foam "miraculous" is also what makes it one of the least profitable commodities to store and transport. As a result, foam products have increasingly been banned from municipal recycling programs in recent years, contributing to their growing presence in landfills and waterways.[12]

Until recently, the United States avoided some of the challenges involved in EPS recycling by shipping up to 70 percent of its recyclable plastics to China. This practice was made possible by low shipping and labor costs and a high demand for recycled materials in China's growing manufacturing industries.[13] Through an efficient system of exchange referred to in the shipping industry as "reverse haulage," the discarded byproducts of American materialism—including large quantities of foam packaging—were routinely shipped back across the ocean in the very same cargo vessels that once carried Chinese consumer goods abroad.[14] These containers full of containers making their way across the Pacific Ocean presents an unlikely parallel to the floating blocks of foam in the Dow Chemical photographs. They signal yet another space of translation, where the

12 Michael Corkery, "Your Foam Coffee Cup Is Fighting for Its Life," *The New York Times*, February 10, 2020.
13 Karen McVeigh, "Huge rise in US plastic waste shipments to poor countries following China ban," *The Guardian*, October 5, 2018.
14 Kate O'Neill, *Waste* (Cambridge: Polity Press, 2019): 156.

materials held within undergo a change of state—from waste back to commodity again as foam's material footprint continues to be traded further and further afield.

The political economist Kate O'Neill describes the expanding global networks of plastic waste through the economic concept of "externalities."[15] By designating waste as an externality, or a byproduct to be disposed of, we continue to deny its existence by pushing it outside of our immediate field of vision—out of sight, out of mind, and even beyond national borders. In December 2017, China implemented a series of policy changes under the title "Operation National Sword," which put a stop to the global circulation of waste, focusing its efforts in particular on limiting the import of plastic waste. The decision had an immediate ripple effect in the global recycling industry. Soon, containers full of discarded plastics piled up in ports and at recycling centers in Europe and around the US, as states and municipalities began implementing cuts to their already limited recycling programs.[16] Without a viable end market for recycling or reuse, over 80 percent of EPS foam products consumed in the United States are currently discarded every year, according to some estimates, occupying up to 30 percent of the total volume of active landfills.[17] Gathered in these quantities at the end of its useful life span, the unintended effects of foam products provide this ubiquitous material with a new kind of visibility. Freed from formal and functional demands, EPS foam re-emerges as a palpable spatial and material problem to be confronted on its own terms.

As a material that speaks in contradictions, EPS foam is perhaps best characterized by its ability to trouble existing categories. It appears disposable, and yet it is very hard to throw away. It is the building block of energy-efficient construction, as well as one of the most visible culprits of the environmental crimes of the plastics industry. Caught between these tensions, EPS foam raises a central question around the unruly afterlives of synthetic materials. What happens when materials that were designed to fulfill stop being subservient to human desires?

15 Ibid., 17.
16 Cheryl Katz, "Piling Up: How China's Ban on Importing Waste Has Stalled Global Recycling," Yale Environment 360, March 7, 2019. Accessed September 10, 2020. https://e360.yale.edu/features/piling-up-how-chinas-ban-on-importing-waste-has-stalled-global-recycling/.
17 Manu Chandra, Colin Kohn, Jennifer Pawlitz, and Grant Powell, "Real Cost of Styrofoam," Saint Louis University, November 22, 2016, https://greendiningalliance.org/wp-content/uploads/2016/12/real-cost-of-styrofoam_written-report.pdf.

Even though foam products did not enter the public's imagination until the second half of the 20th century, the notion that they have a short history is misleading. Like other petroleum-based synthetics of its generation, EPS foam is the product of millions of years of material accumulation, which will in turn take thousands of years to break down. In other words, it is a human-made material that exists beyond human life spans and historical time frames. Read in these terms, it might be more productive to conceive of it less as a thing of the air and more as a thing of the ground—a material with geological implications.

In the field of paleoclimatology, the concept of "proxy data" is used to describe physical records in the natural environment that offer clues to historic patterns of climate variability. Through an analysis of the visible characteristics of tree rings and ice cores, scientists are able to retrace changes in temperature, precipitation, wind patterns, and even cataclysmic events like volcanic eruptions.[18] The nine EPS foam columns on display inside the Chicago pedway described at the opening of this essay provide an analogous record to the patterns of production and consumption that shape our relationship with the material world. Through them, the material residues of the plastics industry can be read as a kind of fossil record, a repository of oil and its effects that evokes what artist Pam Longobardi calls the "cultural archaeology of our time."[19] By placing EPS foam on display as a found material with a history, a footprint, and a will of its own, they offer a tangible medium for reflecting on the literal and symbolic weight of modern materials.

18 Shannon Mattern, "The Big Data of Ice, Rocks, Soils, and Sediments," *Places Journal*, November 2017. Accessed May 12, 2020. https://doi.org/10.22269/171107. See also: Jan Zalasiewicz et al., "The Technofossil Record of Humans," *The Anthropocene Review* 1, no. 1 (April 1, 2014): 34-43.
19 Pam Longobardi, "The Ocean Gleaner," *Drain (Junk Ocean)*, vol. 13, no. 1 (2016).

FULFILLED
Michelle Chang

In February, I hired a young actress named Joelle to play the part of a young architect. She had experience acting as a princess, so I thought she would fit the role. After she sent me a screen test, my only reply was to appear less excited, which seemed strange to her, but she took the note anyway.

A few weeks prior, Ashley Bigham had invited me to participate in a symposium on "material fulfillment." Money was wired to me to pay for my flight and services. This covered Joelle's fees, as well as the cost of a Bluetooth earbud, script, hair clip, and blue collared shirt.

If you meet Joelle, there's little chance you'll mistake her for a Taiwanese architect (there were no Asian actresses-for-hire within a 100-mile radius of Columbus). But from far away—let's say, from the distance projected by an Instagram live feed—she might look like one because of her haircut.

ACT I
SCENE I

An architecture school in Columbus, Ohio. ARCHITECTS are milling around in a large
room, talking to each other and looking at objects in an exhibition. MICHELLE walks
into the gallery.

INT. KNOWLTON SCHOOL OF ARCHITECTURE - NIGHT.

     MICHELLE
     Wow. So much nicer than the pictures.

She gestures generally in the direction of the ceiling.

     ARCHITECT
     Yeah, it's a really great building. Mack and Merrill really know what
     they're doing.

     MICHELLE
     I'll say.

She stands in line and waits to get a cup of wine.

     Red, please.

Architects walk around the gallery slowly, pausing to look at the
boxes on display. She stands next to Ashley and Erik and points to one of
the boxes.

     MICHELLE
     (impersonating Brad Pitt)
     What's in the booox?

Ashley and Erik exchange glances. They walk towards someone they know.

ACT II
SCENE I

An architecture school in Columbus, Ohio. ARCHITECTS are chatting in a large room
and looking at their phones. MICHELLE walks into the lecture hall. She sits in
the second row and listens to ASHLEY introduce the symposium. When her name is
mentioned, she nods and gives a slight wave. She checks emails and Instagram on
her phone when the first panel sets up. She crosses her arms and legs as she
listens to the first panel.

INT. KNOWLTON SCHOOL OF ARCHITECTURE - DAY.

                    MICHELLE
                    (whispering to the person next to her)
                    That was a good one.

She quietly gets up to get a cup of coffee and sits back down.
She blows on the coffee to cool it down and takes a sip.

SCENE II

An almost empty lecture hall. While everyone is finishing lunch,
MICHELLE checks her presentation file with AV PERSON. She holds out
a thumb drive.

                    MICHELLE
                    Can I test this out?

                    AV PERSON
                    Sure.

AV Person takes the thumb drive and connects it to the laptop.

                    AV PERSON
                    Where's the file?

                    MICHELLE
                    Oh, I think it's in the OSU folder. It's called,
                    "Chang Fulfilled."

                    AV PERSON
                    The PowerPoint file?

                    MICHELLE
                    Yeah, that's it. Can I just cycle through to make sure
                    everything works?

                    AV PERSON
                    Knock yourself out.

She copies the file to the desktop and is startled when the computer
makes a sound. She opens the file in presentation mode. After
pressing the arrow key five times, she closes the program.

                    MICHELLE
                    Thanks.

She takes out the thumb drive and walks away.

SCENE III

A full lecture hall. MICHELLE sits in the first row and listens to
ASHLEY introduce the panel. When her name is mentioned, MICHELLE nods
and gives a slight wave. She checks her emails and Instagram on her
phone as the second panel sets up. She sips a cup of coffee as she
listens to the first two speakers. She walks up to the podium to give

her presentation.

INT. KNOWLTON SCHOOL OF ARCHITECTURE – DAY.

      MICHELLE
      (opening her file)
      Ashley, thank you for putting all of this together and for
      inviting me. It's wonderful to have a chance to think about
      what constitutes fulfillment in our line of work. And for this
      panel specifically, how to materially register the contracts
      we make.

      (beat)
      Lately, I've been clocking in a fair number of frequent flier
      miles. With everything that's going on in the news, I've been
      trying to figure out how to run my practice in a way that
      creates a smaller carbon footprint. Since this panel is on
      quote, "finite resources and aesthetic artifacts," it seemed
      as good a chance as any to test out ways architectural work
      (including academic work) can fulfill promises without compro-
      mising quality. To me, that's a representational problem.
      That being said, I hope you'll allow me to try something out.

      (beat)
      So I have to admit, it took me a while to think of what to
      write for this. The characterization of desire in Ashley's
      prompt intrigued me, so I decided to focus on that.

      (beat)
      Here is a still from the 1988 movie, *Who Framed Roger Rabbit*.
      Jessica Rabbit, who you see here on the left, exhibits many
      characteristics typically associated with male desire. But
      what I'd like to draw your attention to is her hair — you
      never get to see the right side of her face because of it.
      In a sense, it denies symmetry …

      (draws a circle around face with index finger)
      … by denying the whole, it creates desire. I'm showing this to
      get more specific about ways in which my work engages desire,
      and it's not this. Well, hopefully it's not.

      As a counterpoint, to the right is a still from the video,
      How Not to Be Seen, made 25 years later. You can see the
      artist Hito Steyerl erasing herself by slowly rubbing her
      face. A true effacing. Using the technique of chroma keying,
      or applying pigment to herself in real space, she assimi-
      lates her image into the virtual space of the camera. Maybe we
      can call that the subject/object becoming part of its context
      and context becoming part of the subject/object. It's like
      lighting a candle, this gradual blurring creates a different
      kind of desire from knowing that the whole can never be
      recovered. To be more specific, let's call that "longing."

      Today I'm going to show two projects that are characterized
      by longing. On one hand, they're way …

      (stretching arms out)

… *too long.* I mean that literally: both relating to time and scale. On the other, they aim to create an effect best described in Michael Hays's 2010 book, *Architecture's Desire.* He writes, "the workings of architecture's desire" lie in "the impossibility of architecture's full realization."

(beat)
This first project is an installation in Los Angeles and is curated and supported by the arts and architecture organization Materials & Applications. It's called *Scoring, Building.* Here it is inside the courtyard at Schindler's Mackey Apartments.

(pointing to the screen)
… this green-colored rectangle here.

(beat)
Materials & Applications put out a competition in 2018 called Staging Construction. It asked participants to "explore construction as both a practice and a performance." Thinking about that, the design for *Scoring, Building* took on construction as a representational issue. What I mean is that the project was designed through a score instead of let's say a plan or a 3D model. The score is a series of graphic and written instructions for a builder. To put it together, I was looking at two kinds of documents: first, material installation guides written by trade associations and companies like USG, and second, project management schedules.

Those two formats together helped me play with construction methods and material artifacts.

(beat)
Here's an example of the first part of the score.

(pointing to right side of slide)
You can see some typical methods culled from the material guides …

(pointing to left side of slide)
… and a drawing of each of these steps as a notational plan. These numbers …

(pointing)
… relate to the written instructions. Here's a part of it. So, let's say establishing the footprint of the pavilion involves laying down a gypsum panel, see 1.1.2. And then repeating that over and over again produces a grid, as you can see in 1.1.3.

(beat)
For the pacing of these instructions, I got really into something called "location-based scheduling." Most projects use action-based scheduling — think Gantt charts and task-oriented spreadsheets — but location-based scheduling organizes construction according to spaces. Really repetitive projects, like towers that can be built floor by floor, make sense for this way of working. Here's the schedule for *Scoring, Building.*

Characteristics, properties, or performance of materials or systems herein described are based on information obtained under controlled test conditions and are for defined architectural end users. JaJa Co. and its member companies make no warranties or other representations as to their characteristics, properties, or performance under any variation from such conditions or in uses in actual construction.

Figure 1: Snapping

LV 83U02.50 Vigorously shake the case to loosen the chalk and ensure the string is uniformly coated. Affix the pushpin or metal hook at starting point A of your line. Release an appropriate amount of string to point B to complete the line. Hold the case over point B, then grab the string with two fingers and pull the line taut. For the best results, snap the line as close to the center of the two points as possible.

Figure 2: Scoring, Breaking

GA 216 4.5.1 Gypsum panel products shall be cut [...] by scoring and breaking. When scoring, a sharp knife shall be used to cut through the gypsum panel product face and into the core. The gypsum panel product shall then be snapped back away from the cut face. The back liner [...] shall be cut or shall be broken by snapping the gypsum panel product in the reverse direction.

Figure 3: Framing

LV: Lee Valley
NGCCG: National Gypsum Company Construction Guide

NGCCG 314 Align floor and ceiling tracks to ensure plumb partition. Secure track with suitable fasteners at a maximum of 24 in. (610 mm) o.c. [...] Install steel studs with all flanges pointed in the same direction. Secure studs located adjacent to door and window frames, partition intersections and corners with 3/8 in. (9.5 mm) pan head Type S screws. Drive screws through both flanges of studs and tracks or by using a stud clincher.

Figure 5: Affixing

USG J371.6 Space screws a maximum of 12" apart on ceilings, 16" on walls and at least 3/8" from ends and edges of panels. Sink screws to just below the panel surface, leaving the paper intact. Use an electric screwgun equipped with an adjustable screw depth control head and Phillips bit. If an electric drill is used, be careful not to overdrive screws.

Figure 6: Finishing

GA 216.19 Taping and finishing shall be done using the hand tools designed for this purpose, such as broad knives or trowels with straight and true edges, or mechanical tools designed for this purpose. The second coat shall be applied with tools of sufficient width to extend approximately 3 ½ in. (90 mm) beyond the center of the joint center. Compound shall be drawn down to a smooth even plane. All levels of finish shall be applied as specified by the designer appropriate to the final decoration.

GA: United States Gypsum Association
USG: United States Gypsum Corporation

▲ Installation instructions for *Scoring, Building* at Mackey Apartments in Los Angeles, for Materials & Applications (2020). Courtesy of JaJa Co.

(beat)
On the horizontal axis is linear feet and on the vertical axis is time. Something that typically takes a couple of weeks to build is extended to a month and a half. Every step — marking, framing, sheathing, programming, etc. — is repeated again and again. There's an inflection point a little more than halfway through, when the whole thing comes together. It's kind of like this:

Long pause.

(beat)
There was a brief moment in mid-February where you could see the pavilion fully formed before it started to break down.

(beat)
This of course couldn't be done in normal circumstances. But the installation format let me test what could be done with a really long project. Some of the material implications were that repetitive cutting or mudding with time-based dyes made the facture of construction a design element.

(beat)
So, for example, an excessive amount of mudding gave the project's massing a different reading.

(beat)

Le Corbusier once allegedly said that you know something
is architecture when a window is too big or too small.
I'm paraphrasing Eisenman's recounting in his 1982 debate
with Christopher Alexander. Eisenman says,

(impersonating Peter Eisenman)
"Once [the window] was the right size it was no longer functioning. When it is the right size, that building is merely
a building …" [ref]

(as Michelle)
Ouch.

(impersonating Peter Eisenman)
"The only way in the presence of architecture that is that
feeling, that need for something other, when the window was
either too large or too small."

(as Michelle)
Who knows what he means by too large or small; but, what it
suggests is that architecture has a role in pushing back
against what appears "just right" — that architecture somehow
inhabits the absence that an unfulfilled expectation forms.
To me, this is a wonderful expression of longing. It's a senti-
ment that Bernard Tschumi captures when he associates with
"architecture that asserts itself as something emergent rather
than final, something that we have to strain to keep in focus
and, even then, hold only momentarily, just before it slips out
of our perception and in the instant it is already lost."

(beat)
If the first project was about longing through scheduling,
the second one tries to get at that by borrowing a local
approach to materials.

(beat)
The second project is a studio and gallery in suburban
Virginia.

(beat)
Oh wow, that's really blown out.

(beat)
Okay, that's better. Like so many other American suburbs, the
area is rich with scalar contrasts. Big box stores often face
small shops and single-family homes commonly look onto malls.
Rather than to understand this vernacular merely as fast and
cheap, this project appreciates it as an American attitude
toward scale.

(beat)
Taken this way, big box stores exhibit a surprising amount of
architectural imagination. Look closely, and one can see the
vestiges of architectural elements in their cladding. Roofs
are frequently flattened into false fronts, paneling systems,
or even layers of paint; façades allude to domestic propor-
tions to break up the monotony of vast scales. The effect is

a building type that tries to hide its bigness.

(beat)
This project, Studio—Gallery, is a building that tries to hide its smallness. Its exterior is clad in a cement-board rainscreen, rendering the light frame construction into a monolithic form. Its massing has a long proportion that exaggerates its scale with two short and two very long facades.

(beat)
Similar to this condition.

(pointing to slide)
The building's front face is less than 20 feet wide. And the sides are about 76 feet.

(beat)
Openings on the north side bring daylight into what appears on the south side as a closed box. And on the interior, two suspended walls divide a shed-like room to carry natural light deep into the gallery.

(beat)
The building site is a corner lot with a parallelogram shape.

(gesturing horizontally)
This direction faces a busy street that divides areas of extra-large and extra-small buildings. South of the site are several chain stores — Super Walmart, Best Buy, Target — and to the north is a middle-class residential neighborhood. The geometry of the lot is a product of the grains on these two opposing sides.

(beat)
The client is a local gallerist and painter. She was a long-time owner of a local gallery, now retired, and has since decided to scale down and focus on painting. In discussing the project, she requested a private building, given the proximity to the big stores.

Long pause.

I guess what I'm trying to do is to get this building to fit in. Um, the project's a private art studio and gallery, so it doesn't really belong here. Its program is out of place; it's neither commercial like the malls nor residential.

So, to blend the studio with its surroundings, it borrows material strategies from its context. In the Steyerl video I mentioned earlier, the subject/object and the environment blurred together through a slow erasure. That doesn't quite fit here, so a better example might be this …

(beat)
… the 1983 Woody Allen movie, *Zelig*. In the film, Allen plays a kind of neurotic shapeshifter. Called a "chameleon man,"

the main character Leonard Zelig assumes the identity of everyone he's with. So, becoming a Chinese version of himself around Asians (as you see here), becoming a psychiatrist version of himself around his psychiatrist, becoming a jazz musician, a baseball player, etc. Zelig desperately wants to blend into his surroundings. So, in a way, the story is about how somebody becomes somebody else, and also what is required to do so.

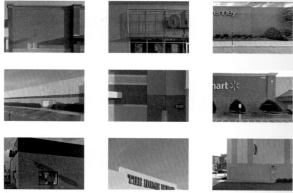

⋏ Chesapeake Big Box Cladding Vernacular. *Studio–Gallery* (2020). Courtesy of JaJa Co.

(beat)
Architecturally speaking, suburban buildings often play a similar game. Elements like pitched roofs and porches are designed to diminish the scales of global chain stores and big banks. Material is applied to signal programs, specifically domestic ones. Rarely do we see buildings scaling the other way.

(beat)
In the movie, Zelig badly wants to be more than he is; he changes his physical appearance *and* personality to become part of his context. What I love about this film is that it's done not only representationally through his clothes and makeup, but also ontologically. Similarly, Studio–Gallery tries to *appear* as more than it is by using large panels and a solid façade, and it attempts to *become* more commercial by privileging the gallery program.

(beat)
Architecture of longing is not a solution so much as a negation of something in the current moment. I wanted to talk about the topic of longing not just because I'm a sucker for the 87-minute take in *Russian Ark*, the plans for Libeskind's Jewish Museum, and the 10-hour-long YouTube format. I think longing does something that reveals a fundamentally hopeful aspect of architecture, which is its capacity to push back against material gratification. And to provoke questions like, in the words of Peggy Lee, "Is that all there is?"

(beat)
Thank you.

Michelle sits back down in the first row and listens to the next speakers.

SCENE IV

A full lecture hall. Michelle sits with ARCHITECTS on her panel and awaits the start of the discussion.

Architect says something about materials. Architect asks Michelle a question. After pausing to think, she starts to speak.

       MICHELLE
       (holding a mic)
       In many ways, I agree with you. But,…

       That's a really great question. If I'm understanding you
       correctly, you're asking if …

       Honestly, I don't know if I know the answer to that question …

She places the mic on the table and crosses her legs. As Architect speaks, she nods her head.

The question and answer session to the panel closes, and the audience applauds. Michelle leaves the lecture hall.

END

▲ Model, *Studio—Gallery* (2020). Courtesy of JaJa Co.

CLEANING UP
Miles Gertler

ʌ *Three Ordinary Funerals* at the 2017 Seoul International
Biennale of Architecture and Urbanism in Seoul, Korea. Photo:
Common Accounts (2017). Courtesy of Common Accounts.

I'll use the word *putrid* as an entry point. The word appears to have emerged in its modern form in the 15th century. It's a compound descriptor in that it communicates both a material state of decomposition and the smell emitted in the process. Fittingly, one can trace its origins to two related but distinct words in Latin: *putris*, which means "rotten, or crumbling," and *putere*, "to stink." Its deeper etymology is shared across language, and the Proto-Indo-European root **puH-* can be found in Sanskrit, Lithuanian, Ancient Greek, and Old Norse. Google Book's online Ngram Viewer presents a steep decline in the use of *putrid* from the 1700s onward—despite a slight uptick around the year 2000—but one might surmise from its graph that we enjoy an 800 percent decrease in our collective exposure to *putridity* today than we did, say, in the year 1800.[1]

The fragrant *potpourri* demonstrates the word's dual connotation. *Potpourri*, literally a "putrid pot" in French, describes the fragrant mixture of dried flora, oils, and herbs kept in a bowl or bag used to scent the home. Rather than disposing of flowers past their prime, *potpourri* aims to circumvent the decomposition of their petals through dehydration, and then uses them as a surface to radiate other fragrances applied later on. The "putrid pot," then, is something of a misnomer, since the mixture therein is paused in its decay and its smell perfumed. It seeks to expand on the perceived aesthetic value of flora through the extension of their olfactory performance. In that sense, *potpourri* is a little like a made-up corpse in an open casket. The body, in blush, eyeshadow, and lipstick—embalmed and quite certainly dead—is still made to perform to some extent as though it were alive.

The very existence of these fragrant little bundles suggests that the putrid holds a strange human appeal. Indeed, this is what the zoologists Robert Dudley and Dustin Stephens proposed in *The Drunken Monkey Hypothesis* in 2000 at the University of California, Berkeley. They argue that, along with our primate ancestors, humans have an innate evolutionary appreciation for the fetid vapors of fermenting fruit and that for millennia, sensitive noses have embraced the scent of rot to guide us to abundant food sources in the humid tropics where humans first emerged.

As our exposure to the rotting and malodorous has generally diminished, so too have the strange pleasures and diverse forms of

1 "Putrid," Google Books Ngram Viewer: 1800-2019, Accessed November 19, 2020: https://books.google.com/ngrams/graph?content=putrid&year_start=1800&year_end=2019.

value that a nearness to the perverse, unpleasant, and putrid once brought. Much of the work in the office that I co-direct with Igor Bragado, Common Accounts, deals with this issue. We began examining the future of the material business of death as students and have since staged a number of installations, pavilions, and exhibitions that posit the material dimension of self-design as a pragmatic tool for city building. This means that, occasionally, we encounter substances of a putrid nature.

Our inquiry into death began with a survey of the industry in the contemporary landscape—indeed, *deathcare* is an industry. Who are the experts in the management of death? There are hospital groups and funeral providers and cemetery chains that are perhaps most visible, but early on, we became fascinated by the protocol logic of the US Military's Department of Mortuary Affairs: the unit that manages the retrieval, identification, ceremonialization, and return of human remains and personal effects from the theater of war. Theirs is a system that extends to the infrastructural and logistical, layers of memorial and ceremony that consider issues of performance and image. Field guides define both how to cover a given search area in service of retrieving a body and how the boots of the honor guard should march in choreography across the tarmac at Dover Air Force Base—the military's lone American port mortuary.[2] Mortuary Affairs documents catalog how many bags of ice are needed to surround a cadaver in trans-Atlantic flight and how the aluminum transfer case ought to be enrobed in a flag.[3] In their pages, one can learn how the uniforms of dead soldiers should be pressed and fitted; how the media bus that ferries press photographers to view "dignified transfers" at Dover is oriented to shield grieving family

A golden curtain shrouds the alkaline hydrolysis system inside *Three Ordinary Funerals* at the 2017 Seoul International Biennale of Architecture and Urbanism in Seoul, Korea. Photo: Common Accounts (2017). Courtesy of Common Accounts.

---

2 "This manual implements Air Force Policy Directive (AFPD) 36-26, Total Force Development. It describes the movements and procedures for saluting, drill, ceremonies, reviews, and parades." *Air Force Manual 36-2203.* (Department of the Air Force, November 2013): 1.
3 *Joint Publication 4-06.* Mortuary Affairs, Department of the Air Force. October 2011.

members from their lenses. To borrow the language of Andres Jaque, Mortuary Affairs promotes a "transurban," performance of death that links remote situations as an ensemble, and sees opportunity for ceremony in every logistical gesture.[4] That is, concerns of a scientific, forensic, cultural, and political nature and the actors who channel them are not only rendered visible in complex events serving multiple, disparate audiences, but are mobilized toward the fulfillment of each other's desires (the press truck offering the family privacy, while also enabling the funeral's broader viewership with the tarmac as backdrop and necessary platform to receive the flight).

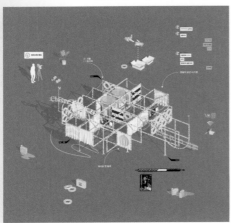

↗ Adaptation of the Ceremonial Spaceframe from *Three Ordinary Funerals* for the National Museum of Modern and Contemporary Art, Korea. Common Accounts (2018). Courtesy of Common Accounts.

For the inaugural Seoul Biennale of Architecture and Urbanism in 2017, exhibition co-directors Alejandro Zaera-Polo and Hyungmin Pai commissioned Common Accounts to materialize some of our early work on death. Igor and I proposed a prototypical funeral home centered around the management of both the virtual and human remains of the dead. One of the more novel and increasingly plausible alternatives in remains disposition, or disposal, is a process called alkaline hydrolysis. It has been branded by one provider in the industry as flameless, or "liquid cremation." Through an hours-long process, the body is liquified into a fertile solution and dissolved into its constituent amino acids, sugars, peptides, and salts in a lye bath. This entire process takes place in a pressurized steel container with an internal temperature of about 300 degrees Fahrenheit. The pressure is so great that the doors and gaskets on some of these instruments are manufactured in facilities that produce similar parts for military submarines.

Alkaline hydrolysis has been in use for decades as a simple

---

4 Andres Jaque has developed the concept of "transurbanism" in texts and projects like *Transurban Love* (The Seoul Biennale of Architecture and Urbanism, 2017), and design studios he has led at Columbia GSAPP and Princeton University, like the Transurban States of America (2015). Here we acknowledge the term's description of situations that are physically remote, yet which have immediate and often reflexive impact on one another due to the technological bridging of distance through easy digital communication, shared cultural milieu, interwoven economic engagement, and layered infrastructural linkage. In other words, societies that function seamlessly, unobstructed by geographical distance, that in turn produce many of the effects of "urban milieu" without the prerequisite of spatial consolidation.

organic chemistry to break down unneeded animal tissues in large-scale agricultural operations and in biology labs as a convenient means of disposal for the remains of test subjects. It has recently been touted as an ecological alternative to cremation since it requires a fraction of the energy and involves no combustion. Its most fervent proponents argue that the fluid human remains that result from the process are stable and safe to flush down ordinary sewage systems. Further, the liquid constitutes a super concentrated fertilizer. An early adopter of the technology for human remains disposition in Ontario told us about a new collaboration between his funeral home and a nearby marijuana producer. They had recently begun experimenting with the effluence in their greenhouses—that was about a year before the funeral home in question was shut down.

Alkaline hydrolysis is largely unregulated as a novel technology in deathcare, and, as such, many regulatory bodies are playing catch up, temporarily shutting facilities that offer the service while they conduct the testing and analysis required to enforce their safe operation. After all, dead bodies can contain pathogens and substances that pose a risk to those who come into contact with them. Remains disposition is meant not only to compact and manage the body as a problem of storage, but also to neutralize the biological activity therein.

Liquid cremation is not currently legal for human funerals in Korea, but we located a producer of alkaline hydrolysis systems for other uses a few hours south of Seoul—Supreme Thermal Instrument—who offered to loan us one of their machines for our funeral simulation. They were eager to assist in opening up the conversation around the design of death, in order to foster an expansion of their technology's legal applications.

In a country of roughly 50 million people, one fifth of South Korea's population lives in Seoul, and more than 80 percent live in cities countrywide. Although three quarters of the population identify as Christian or Atheist, many of South Korea's cultural traditions around death are still informed by Confucian heritage. Since the Korean war, Seoul has urbanized so

Visitors engage with the alkaline hydrolysis system in a still image from a short film of *Three Ordinary Funerals* prepared for the Cube Museum of Design in Kerkrade, the Netherlands. Video photography: Jong Wook Choi (2017). Editing and graphics: Andrew Gilbride (2019). Courtesy of Common Accounts and the Cube Museum.

extensively that most single-story residential neighborhoods and *hanok* courtyard houses where funerals were once held have been leveled to make way for higher density development. As a result of this, both the location and form of funerals in Seoul have become a subject for redesign in the last few decades. The development of the city has also minimized available land for burial, which 30 years ago was the only acceptable means of remains disposition in the country.

Still image from a short film of *Three Ordinary Funerals* prepared for the Cube Museum of Design in Kerkrade, the Netherlands. Video photography: Jong Wook Choi (2017). Editing and graphics: Andrew Gilbride (2019). Courtesy of Common Accounts and the Cube Museum.

Our site was a neighborhood of recently refurbished *hanoks* near Seodaemun Station, not far from the symbolic locus of Gwanghwamun and Gyeongbokgung Palace. In addition to the machine, Supreme Thermal Instrument provided several gallons of the liquid animal remains typically processed with their instruments for remains disposition at laboratory and agricultural facilities for us to use to stage the simulation and irrigate a memorial garden suspended above the funeral home.

The government-funded Korean National Council for Cremation Promotion was established to popularize incineration of the body as a suitable alternative. Around the year 2000, the Council embarked on a multi-pronged marketing effort to sell the concept of cremation to a public skeptical of any action that might degrade the perceived physical integrity of the dead, as per the Confucian tenets on the subject. This effort included pressuring popular soap operas to relocate on-screen funerals to the crematoria and funeral halls of urban hospitals that had cropped up as traditional sites became scarce. The government had also helped fund the construction of these new spaces, which have altogether contributed to the $2.3 billion industry managed in large part by healthcare giants like Samsung, Hyundai, and their affiliates. Some of these spaces are reminiscent of airports in their scale and automation and leave little space for personalization or intimacy.

When we arrived to begin installation in August of 2017, the *hanok* neighborhood earmarked for the biennale was being renovated to serve as a youth hostel and exhibition venue; the paint was still wet, and electricians were still busy at work in many of the neighboring houses. Our alkaline hydrolysis machine arrived on the back of a truck a couple weeks ahead of the opening and was lowered into the courtyard of the *hanok* by crane. We occupied the last house on our block, fronting on a large boundary road, which made crane use possible. The fluid arrived at the same time in six clear rubber jugs. We set them aside while the rest of the structure came together.

A steel frame was built around the hydrolysis machine and anchored into a buried foundation. This structure—a composition of nearly 30 one-meter by one-meter cubic frames welded together from fine metal members—hosted an arsenal of ceremonial infrastructure. From its limbs, floating lightly a couple meters above the tiled roof of the *hanok*, hung flags, planting boxes, and bright-yellow ropes, slung as if from stanchions, connoting a dignified realm beyond which something significant (but also infrastructural, as suggested by their neon coloring) was taking place. Hoisted on semi-circular segments of the frame were slogans that read "Closer Each Day" in English and Korean letters, and at the frame's center were tanks fed by the output of the hydrolysis system below. The curtain of gold fabric that shrouded the machine in the middle of the courtyard hung from a pill-shaped track suspended from the steel frame's underbelly. In all, the structure was supported on six slim circular steel columns, two of which landed on the outside of one wing of the *hanok*, framing its entrance on the alleyway. As visitors entered they passed through a clear rubber curtain that read "No Philias, No Phobias. You Are Entering A Funeral."

Inside the home, we simulated a virtual afterlife upload portal. A television screened the online crowdsourcing of a digital archive. Here, the giga-remains of the urban dead would be gathered by a community of online peers into a memorial vault, and message boards would showcase notes and RIPs. Since this was a funeral, someone had to "die." We worked with Dasol Han, a designer based in Seoul, to produce a fictional character whose simultaneous and authentic online avatars were all memorialized at this funeral along-side her corporeal remains, hence the title, *Three Ordinary Funerals*.

When we first began working on death, we naively imagined a complete and perpetual collection of one's life materialized by and shared among the community of the deceased. In a post–Cambridge Analytica, post-election meddling, post-Equifax leak, post-your-parents'-generation-ruining-Facebook world, we imagined instead a complete and perpetual collection of one's life locked away irretrievably in a vault of unknown design: a black box.

▲   The virtual afterlife upload portal inside *Three Ordinary Funerals* at the 2017 Seoul International Biennale of Architecture and Urbanism in Seoul, Korea. Photo: Common Accounts (2017). Courtesy of Common Accounts.

While the upload portal fostered mourning online, the structure of the funeral home would make death visible at the scale of the neighborhood—part of a larger strategy to atomize deathcare across the city and enable citizen groups to reclaim the social, ecological, and material value that harnessing death could provide. Take for example the case of Abbey Stadium Sports Centre in Worcestershire, England. In 2013 the Redditch Borough Council began heating the Abbey Stadium swimming pool with excess heat diverted from the crematorium nearby. This in turn reduced the leisure center's carbon footprint by cutting the pool's heating costs by 42 percent. It also granted to the community a sensuous and pleasurable experience via death's productive outputs and yielded to the dead a final act of civic generosity and public engagement. To strategize how our project might engage the public and yield similar opportunities for the production of value from death, we engaged the expertise of Seoul-based curator Jihoi Lee who, as our research and project manager, helped adapt our earlier work in death to this new context and link us to local planners, consultants, and industry specialists.

We spent several days on the outskirts of Seoul in peak-summer heat, hand-painting a black and white floral graphic onto the steel armature that was designed to emerge from the *hanok* courtyard. The motif was an abstraction of chrysanthemums and other flowers with significance in local funerary traditions; we stenciled this neo-*potpourri* across every limb of what we called *The Ceremonial Spaceframe*. This motif was inspired in part by an interview Igor and I had conducted two years earlier with Patrick Burke, Michael Graves's deputy on the Swan and Dolphin Hotel. Shortly after Michael Graves had died, Burke told us how the Princeton Architecture Library had received a new monograph on Josef Hoffmann in 1986, around the time that Disney had commissioned the hotel. A crucial condition of Graves's contract with Disney was that the Epcot hotel be thematized—a stipulation that found legal articulation through the term "extraordinary decoration" in the architect's contract with Disney and Tishman Realty. Burke and Graves had just discovered Hoffmann's use of floral patterns, demonstrated in the sketch for a child's room for the house of Ernst Bauer (1927) and in the Austrian Pavilion at the International Exposition of Modern Decorative and Industrial Arts in Paris (1925). Influenced by these precedents and an encounter with Albert Stockdale's iconic *Martinique* banana leaf wallpaper during a design meeting at the Beverly Hills Hotel, Graves's team saw a way forward and a banana leaf paint-by-numbers came to flank the Dolphin Hotel's pyramid, while a wave motif occupied the Swan facade.

We in turn became intrigued with Hoffmann's florals, hence our elaboration of the space frame—a structure made of a three-dimensional grid of square steel tubes—in Seoul. Beyond the painted chrysanthemums, the structure was adorned with nylon floral wreaths and flower boxes to accommodate a suspended garden. The space frame was further equipped with memorial infrastructure— flags, lighting, irrigation tubing, and tanks—we began to decant the fluid remains sent from our sponsor into spray bottles. The idea was that visitors would be free to fertilize the plants that formed the funeral's memorial garden: this being a central physical transmutation of the liquified dead.

The night before the opening, we uncapped one of the five-liter jugs outside our *hanok*, unleashing what can only be described as one of the most putrid odors I've ever encountered.

It was staggeringly potent, harsh in the nostrils and throat, and incontestably biotic—probably not unlike a corpse in active decay.

Granted, it was our understanding that the effluence from the alkaline hydrolysis machine required several rounds of processing and filtering before it became fragrance neutral and adequately diluted for use as a fertilizer. We had seen samples of the fluid remains subjected to varying degrees of post-processing at our sponsor's headquarters several months before and had requested the clearest, champagne-hued version of the juice for our funeral home.

The fluid we received thoroughly embodied *putridity* itself— liquid cremation is after all an accelerated version of a body's natural decomposition—and the scent had not yet been neutralized in the very fresh batch we had procured. Nonetheless, the fertilization of the garden was a centerpiece of the ecological model of funeral we had designed, so we proceeded to decant a liter or so of fluid into three plastic spray bottles. The jugs proved cumbersome and a good amount of the liquid remains cascaded down my hand securing the smaller bottle. The stench hadn't much lessened, and after a few seconds the intensity of the mixture became clear as mild caustic burns began to appear where the fluid had made contact with my skin. Once I had tended to the dermatological situation, we returned to hose down the laneway, which smelled faintly of decomposition well into the next day. We diluted and filled two bottles and resealed the jug. Thus, our funeral home came to life, its hanging gardens constituting a living *potpourri* fostered and only lightly scented by the outputs of death.

When all was set, we turned on the CCTV system, which consisted of two cameras positioned within the steel frame and focused on the planter boxes that hung above the courtyard. These recorded and transmitted the growing of the memorial garden to the virtual afterlife cloud—another of our funeral home's poly-material, re-instantiations of the urban dead. A screen in one of the *hanok*'s ancillary spaces played the live video feed for visitors while a soundtrack of slogans pulled from deathcare industry advertising played on a speaker in the courtyard.

We worked on this project conscious of architecture's long-standing embrace of a less corporeal approach to dying. It seemed to us that it had been several decades since our profession had seriously considered death beyond the poetics and metaphysical dimension fostered in the mid-century and post-modernism; and yet, more people are living and therefore also dying today in greater densities than ever before, which is becoming a problem for large cities everywhere.

While Aldo Rossi, John Hejduk, Carlo Scarpa, and Gunnar Asplund emphasized the spatial and narrative poetry of their columbaria, cemeteries, and crematoria, other industries stepped in to design the technological aspects of deathcare, resulting in a hygienic distancing of death from daily life that was mirrored by architecture's effort to isolate death as an existentially remote state of being. In contrast, deathcare experts like Mortuary Affairs must manage death in a mode that is forced to prioritize the fetid material realities of biological expiration, given the ad hoc conditions that govern their operations.

Encounters with the morbid remind us that design is the mediating technology that keeps our hands shielded from alkaline burns, our digital archives private, and our homes safe from vile odors. What we believe, of course, is that we ought to embrace a radical nearness to those things less comfortable. There are many forms of value and gratification to be yielded from it. Our clients are not simply human, but material, and subject to transformation. Their values and desires can be transmitted and fulfilled through those mutations, if design allows. The material constituents of the urban realm may often be at odds in their agencies, and even more so to our own, but there are valuable co-dependencies to be mined from the opportunities their proximities bring. After all, the heat of the crematorium can be used to fry your eggs; your social media is the new cemetery; and the sale of your surplus tissue could pay the mortgage on your house. And that may be worth getting your hands dirty.

⋀ The ceremonial spaceframe hovers above the *hanok* roof. *Three Ordinary Funerals* at the 2017 Seoul International Biennale of Architecture and Urbanism in Seoul, Korea. Photo: Common Accounts (2017). Courtesy of Common Accounts.

OUT OF FAVOR
Ashley Bigham

⌃ Outpost Office, *Open/Work*, Kharkiv, Ukraine (2019). Photo: Erik Herrmann.
Courtesy of Outpost Office.

The Barabashova market in Kharkiv, Ukraine is a study in architectural paradoxes. A visit begins at the metro stop Akademika Barabashova where shining blue concave tiles cover the walls, neoclassical stone-faced columns line the platform, and celestial light fixtures adorn the ceiling. Constructed in 1984, at the end of the Soviet Brutalist period in Ukraine, this underground station is emblematic of Soviet design at the time—cheerful, optimistic, and highly regulated.[1] The metro station's escalators act as Roman vomitoria, expelling pedestrians from the underground platform directly into the boisterous market above, spewing unassuming visitors into a cacophony of audible and visual noise. In contrast to the bold metro station below, the Barabashova market presents an entirely different dimension of Ukrainian architecture, one born out of the chaotic economic conditions of Eastern Europe during the 1990s following the collapse of the Soviet Union. The market's architecture is not centralized, not standardized, and lacking top-down design guidelines; instead, there are improvised constructions, shared resources, and entangled reciprocity.

To understand the particularity of post-Soviet markets, one must first understand the circulation of consumer goods during the Soviet Union. The waning years of the Soviet Union were marked by material shortages and a growing desire for items manufactured outside the closed network. The difficulty of obtaining these items created a cultural network of alternative methods of procurement, and an enormous amount of time was spent in pursuit of everyday items. Long lines appeared for milk, soap, foreign-made bras, books, televisions, hair dye, and toilet paper; consumers remained in a constant state of uncertainty, torn between work or domestic responsibilities and the time required to queue for goods. The queue became such an important Soviet pastime that it was considered a public ritual, one of negotiation and hierarchies, stories and substitutes.[2] As one former Soviet citizen recounts in Svetlana Alexievich's *Secondhand Time: The Last of the Soviets*, "Our country fell apart from the deficit of women's boots and toilet paper, because of the fact that

---

1 Alex Bykov and Ievgeniia Gubkina, *Soviet Modernism, Brutalism, Post-modernism: Buildings and Structures in Ukraine 1955-1991* (Berlin: DOM, 2019): 13.

2 Vladimir Sorokin, "Farewell to the Queue," afterword to *The Queue*, trans. Jamey Gambrell (New York: New York Review of Books, 2008): 257: "No, it was not only for butter and nails that people stood in endless lines. The queue was a quasi surrogate for church. Through the act of standing up, standing up for, through, and in and on lines (i.e., in all senses of the word 'to stand,' trans.) regularly for several hours, people participated in a sort of ritual, after which, instead of the Eucharist and absolution of their sins, they received foodstuffs and manufactured goods."

there were no oranges. It was those goddamn blue jeans!"[3]

Material shortages and subsequent rationing gave rise to a culture of *blat*, an informal economy of favors that was required to obtain certain goods or services.[4] *Blat* is a personal fulfillment system that relies on peer-to-peer relationships and social networks. Although it may at times be considered unscrupulous, *blat* is not synonymous with corruption. *Blat* is a system for creativity; it flourishes on the margins of a system, or in its absence. It is the productive friction between desires and realities, a manifestation of abutting supply chains and fashionable aspirations. It has even been suggested that the Soviet Union was a highly entrepreneurial society in that it "forced all citizens to become micro-entrepreneurs, to enact entrepreneurship in even the most mundane facets of everyday life."[5] This micro-economic activity became a way for individuals to successfully cope with shortages of consumer goods through self-organization of their material and social relationships. This deeply seated practice of *blat*, like any ritual practice, did not die with the collapse of a nation-state; it remained necessary in many aspects of daily life, and in the case of markets and bazaars, binds informal entrepreneurial activities to architecture: its spaces, physical form, and material compositions.

Barabashova Market was established in 1995, at a time when the Ukrainian economy was struggling and the material circula-

⋏ Vintage clothing and household goods at the flea market Rynok Starykh Rechey in Kharkiv, Ukraine. Ashley Bigham (2020).

⋏ Automotive and mechanical parts for sale at Rynok Barabashova, Kharkiv, Ukraine. Ashley Bigham (2020).

⋏ Sidewalk flower market near Halytsky Rynok in Lviv, Ukraine. Ashley Bigham (2020).

3 Svetlana Alexievich, *Secondhand Time: The Last of the Soviets*, trans. Bela Shayevich (New York: Random House, 2016): 52.
4 According to Alena Ledeneva, *blat* is "an exchange of 'favors of access' in conditions of shortages and a state system of privileges." Alena V. Ledeneva, *Russia's Economy of Favours: Blat, Networking, and Informal Exchange* (Cambridge: Cambridge University Press, 1998): 37.
5 Alf Rehn and Saara Taalas, "'Znakomstva I Svyazi' (Acquaintances and connections) – Blat, the Soviet Union, and mundane entrepreneurship," *Entrepreneurship & Regional Development* 16 no. 3 (August 2004): 235–50. See also Abel Polese and Peter Rogers, "Surviving post-socialism: the role of informal economic practices," *International Journal of Sociology and Social Policy* 31 no. 11/12 (2011): 612–18.

tion of consumer goods had been disrupted following the end of the communist state. Barabashova thrived during this transition economy, and today the market boasts a footprint of over 75 hectares and is considered one of the largest markets in Eastern Europe.[6] It is organized in long, linear, double-sided stretches of open-air shops covered by aluminum frame barrel vault walkways. Parking lots, independent sellers, and bus stops define the market's fuzzy edges. Its many sections are divided by type of goods: household goods, appliances, tools and plumbing, bicycles, building materials, hunting and fishing, fabrics, curtains and carpets, leather and fur, outerwear, footwear, hats, clothing, auto parts, children's toys, etc. The transitions between products can be gradual or abrupt; vegetables are adjacent to meat, while tools and plumbing are near fur coats. Generic storefront wall systems are used to fully enclose some shops while others remain open to the elements, save a translucent polycarbonate roof or a collection of precisely placed sun umbrellas. Bright green, red, or blue tarps are hung, draped, or tied in all the places walls might normally be needed, shielding one from the sun in the summer and the wind in the winter. Cardboard boxes or wooden pallets are fastened together to create sporadic patches of new ground atop cracked pavement. In addition to the namesake metro stop, the market also contains stations for the popular private minibuses known as *marshrutka*, numerous currency exchange booths, a post office, bridal shops, a bank, a medical center, cafes, and public restrooms. With 20,000–40,000 visitors per day, Barabashova Market rivals the size of a small Ukrainian city.

With so many amenities, Barabashova is a self-supporting commercial infrastructure. Every consumer desire can be met, including those of the market employees themselves; mobile carts selling tea, soup, and baked goods are pulled or pushed up and down the long aisles, pausing only when a vendor or odd shopper calls for sustenance. Vendors' lunch breaks are taken without leaving sight of their wares; small groups of women cluster around a neighbor's overturned plastic crate to eat soup, pickles, or cabbage salad, sipping warm tea in their booths encased by walls of leather shoes or bedazzled blue jeans. In addition to consumer goods, the market includes wholesale vendors who sell products marketed directly to other sellers, including the supplies needed to operate a market stall: signs

6 Statistics according to the Barabashova market website, accessed December 20, 2020, https://barabashovo.ua/ua/about.html.

that read "SALE," "BACK IN MINUTES," "HOT TEA COFFEE," "DON'T TOUCH"; plastic coat hangers in fluorescent colors; mannequin heads, torsos, and full bodies; and the ubiquitous white metal gridded screens for displaying objects, which come in various spinning or stationary varieties.

▲ Shipping containers stacked as stalls at the 7th Kilometer Bazaar in Odesa, Ukraine. Ashley Bigham (2020).

As capitalism expands to new territories in post-socialist contexts, shopping spaces record the transformation of economic systems, giving physical characteristics to informal economic relationships. The result is a spliced condition of public and private spaces—markets are mini shopping cities with their own regulations, security forces, currencies, and social hierarchies. The space of shopping is neither democratic nor free; it can require negotiation or provide anonymity. Shopping can lead to regret or disappointment, but also to the fulfillment of desire. As Sharon Zukin has noted, "Cultural theorists are only half right when they say that by choosing products, we create our identity. Our identity is formed by the whole activity of shopping—an activity that we experience as both freedom and necessity."[7] In Ukraine, nearly any material object in the country can be sourced and procured at a bazaar, granted one knows how to find it.

▲ Wholesale vendor supplies at Rynok Barabashova, Kharkiv, Ukraine. Ashley Bigham (2020).

▲ Meat counter at Zhitny Rynok, Kyiv, Ukraine. Ashley Bigham (2020).

This procurement process rarely involves searching a directory, but takes place through a series of face-to-face inquiries in the market as shoppers are directed from one stall to another until they locate their desired wares. Although at first glance these "informal" markets may appear disordered or chaotic, in reality, bazaars are highly ordered, complex systems of collectivity where issues of scarcity are revealed and solved through physical constructions.

Bazaars, open-air markets, and other spaces of informal economic activity exist in many cities worldwide, not only in

7 Sharon Zukin, *Point of Purchase: How Shopping Changed American Culture* (New York: Routledge, 2004): 253.

post-Soviet contexts, but the specificity of Ukrainian bazaars and markets emerges from the particular combination of material objects and their related cultural practices. *Babushkas* selling fresh meat sit behind white-tile counters cleaning their fingernails and sipping tea while resting their arms on hog fat. Two women hold up a sheet to create an impromptu dressing room in a dark corner of a shipping container repurposed as a clothing stall. An elderly man reuses his plastic shopping bag for years, washing and hanging it on a clothes-line to dry when it becomes dirty, filling it with legal documents, or apples, or ice cream he buys at the market. This simple plastic recep-

tacle—a material vestige of *blat*, with a fake Hugo Boss logo—doubles as a briefcase or handbag as he conducts business around town or shops for his grandchildren.

Each object at a bazaar embodies an entire cultural story, one of daily rituals and global supply chains; and in post-communist countries, plastic shopping bags loom large in popular culture and everyday practicality. Under communism, foreign-made plastic bags were a luxury item and an important symbol of Western consumerism and abundance, often brought back from trips abroad and given as gifts to family and friends. In contrast to the disposable posture of the plastic bag in Western Europe, these bags were reused over and over again and carried daily; to carry a plastic bag daily was to be prepared for an unpredicted supply of scarce items that might appear in a shop at a moment's notice.[8] Today, the material legacy

↗ Rynok Barabashova, Kharkiv, Ukraine. Photos: Ashley Bigham (2019).

of the bag endures—if not its original purpose—and bazaars are filled with vendors selling sturdy plastic bags with bright floral patterns, Ukrainian folk art images, exotic landscape scenes, and the classic counterfeit BMW or Hugo Boss logos. In addition to their popularity as practical everyday items and among those nostalgic for the frugalness of a previous generation, plastic bags have captured the attention and cult-following of a diverse population; they have been

8 Leah Valtin-Erwin, "A Bag for All Systems," 2020. (Unpublished essay shared with author, publication pending).

analyzed in doctoral dissertations on consumer culture and even in a recent issue of *Vogue*.[9] How might material practices developed for a plastic bag affect the way a society treats all material objects? Tracing the origins of any particular object in the *blat* supply chain, from invention to cultural popularity to eventual undesirable commodity, offers a promissory note for architecture. What if architectural materials were treated as infinitely reusable as a plastic bag? Might we lovingly pry nails from wooden boards or smuggle aluminum fasteners across international borders?

The architectural materials of bazaars—corrugated aluminum sheets, metal hanging grids, slick white tiles, aluminum-framed awnings, wooden pallets, fabric curtains, polyethylene-coated tarps— are often hidden beneath layers of fabric, stacks of cookware, rows of shoes, or piles of plush toys. These consumer goods provide yet another quality to the architecture of bazaars, one steeped in a partic- ular "material ethics," a term used by Rosalyn Shieh to describe a cultural attitude toward material use.[10] If one were to walk quickly through the sprawling complex of small buildings and temporary structures of Barabashova market, one might come away with the feeling that the market is actually made of products for sale rather than the building materials that support them. The products provide the architecture's character: thousands of individual representationss of its daily maintenance and care. Products are meticulously displayed, arranged, and organized in order to catch the eye of shoppers; even the placement of the seller's body is considered part of the ensemble, often completing the symmetrical arrangement perched on a small stool among a mountain of floral cooking pots or an array of light bulbs. The specific cuts of meats, or variations of plastic house slip- pers, or prevalence of men's handbags, or scarcity of products manu- factured in the European Union are not only determined by regional consumer desires but also legacies of previous economies, ingrained cultural practices, international trade agreements, or cross-border smuggling. In other words, a continually unfolding series of favors.

Throughout the world, architecture is commonly constructed through favors: material exchanges, gifts, reciprocity, or acts of kind- ness. These favors could include zoning variances, tax credits, mate- rial bartering, knowledge sharing, political pressure, or building permits. In many instances, these acts reinforce systems of cronyism

9 Liana Satenstein, "Why Are Pretty Plastic Bags So Popular in Eastern Europe?," *Vogue*, September 5, 2017, https://www.vogue.com/article/popular-plastic-bags-ukraine-eastern-europe.

that characterize most systems of centralized authority. By contrast, the concept of *blat* suggests the possibility of peer-to-peer relationships based on social reciprocity to circumvent repressive institutions. Although *blat* may also be used with harmful consequences, its unique characteristics encourage entrepreneurial methods of material procurement, construction, and reuse. For those who sell and shop in Ukrainian bazaars—the majority of whom are women—informal economic activity and its material manifestations are a profoundly creative platform. It is an architecture that exists outside the hegemony of patronage, a model for design and material procurement that confers agency to individuals outside traditional power structures through alternative channels.

A market such as Barabashova is the manifestation of thousands of individual peer-to-peer negotiations organized in space: *blat* at an architectural scale. It is also emblematic of the broader relationship between the economy of favors and architectural construction in Ukraine. Ukraine's geopolitical status—an independent post-Soviet nation not itself a member of the European Union, but sharing significant borders with several EU member states, Russia, and the Black Sea—creates incentives for informal entrepreneurial activities where larger systems have failed. Ukraine's geographical location, political alliances, and trade agreements (or lack thereof) affect the specific products available to be bought and sold in the country's markets, and in turn, the material ethics cultivated; the curated, careful use of the plastic bag is just one example.

What can understanding *blat* offer architects and designers today? An architecture of *blat* might value the material procurement or construction process over the final form; it might never see a structure as "complete" but always in a state of becoming; it might offer a creative platform for individuals who construct, shape, and curate space as a daily ritual; it might reveal the inherent strangeness of our contemporary material circulation practices; it might highlight the embedded regional bias of global supply chains; it might empower those at the margins of society who use informal econo-

↗ Rynok Barabashova, Kharkiv, Ukraine. Photo: Ashley Bigham (2019).

---

10 According to Shieh, "In place of an aesthetic that represents a culture is an attitude, a material ethics." See Rosalyne Shieh, "It's fine." *Log* 41 (2017): 41.

mies for survival; and it might, as all architecture should, provide delight.

OPEN/WORK

To celebrate the first year of a newly established bachelor's program at the Kharkiv School of Architecture in 2019, Outpost Office—a design practice I co-direct with Erik Herrmann—led a seminar and collaborated with students to curate, design, and fabricate the exhibition *Open/Work*.[11] The exhibition asks, "What *makes* an architecture school?" as a material, curatorial, and pedagogical provocation. The project began by collecting the ephemera of the school itself,

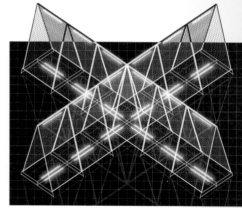

Outpost Office, *Open/Work* (2019). Courtesy of Outpost Office.

objects and materials unique or quotidian, which were used as material evidence of individual and collective pedagogical lessons. Much like the aforementioned consumer objects, each material artifact in the exhibition represents a negotiation of creative inputs, material constraints, and personal desires.

In this challenging context of bricolage—a design-build project at a newly formed school situated within the economic and political context of post-Soviet, post-revolution Ukraine—this exhibition was both an aesthetic project about the display culture at Ukrainian bazaars and a logistical challenge to design using only local materials that were readily available in Kharkiv's bazaars, relying heavily on Barabashova market as the city's largest and most extensive. In other words, we used bazaars as both a practical procurement method and a conceptual framework for design. The goal was not to replicate the aesthetics of bazaars in the design, but to tap into the various forms of design intelligence they present—the grouping of objects and layers of visual information, the readymade infrastructural elements, the uses of social networks and relationships. It became an architecture of favors that relied on the kindness of Uber drivers, security guards, vendors willing to patiently speak a

11 *Open/Work* was a collaborative project including curators and tutors: Ashley Bigham and Erik Herrmann (Outpost Office), Boris Filonenko, and Alina Yesaian; and students: Alisa Aleksandrova, Maria Kolomiytseva, Natalia Kozub, Dmytro Legeyda, Olha Mozgova, Anna Pelypenko, Kateryna Pelypenko, Anna Prokopchuk, Polina Sanzharevska, Anna Sokolova, and Tetyana Telnova. Special thanks to the Kharkiv School team: Oleg Drozdov, Svitlana Rybalko, Oleksandra Naryzhna, Olha Oryshchenko, Yevheniia Dulko, Kuba Snopek, Lawrence Barth, Alexandra Nikitenko, and many others.

little English, Americans with elementary Ukrainian, Kharkiv School administrators, grandmothers who cared for the children of students during class, women who meticulously mopped the floor of the exhibition hall, and many other peripheral actors. Architecture always involves a diverse cast in the building process, yet in this context, we became uniquely aware of the fundamental role played by these peripheral characters and the degree to which our work intertwined with the informal economy of favors.

The white metal screens used as the exhibition's primary material are typically erected by bazaar vendors to densely display their goods. In the exhibition, we used these readymade screens and asked the students to design new attachment details and consider curatorial ideas of organization. The exhibition contained only a few material elements (lights, ceramic tiles, plywood, and metal); and the only connections were zip ties, so that it could be easily disassembled and reassembled later as pin-up boards or other pieces of infrastructure needed by the school. Each material element of the exhibition has continued to be reused in novel and creative constructions in service of the school's mission; for example, plywood tables originally constructed for the exhibition have been reused as working surfaces for students, presentation surfaces for symposia, and informal seating elements.

↟   Outpost Office, *Open/Work*, Kharkiv, Ukraine (2019). Photo: Erik Herrmann. Courtesy of Outpost Office.

Visitors to the exhibition were encouraged to touch, handle, and explore the objects on display, mimicking the ease and tactility of bazaar shopping. Both the act of curation by the students and the act of viewing required a more direct experience of the objects themselves, resulting in improvised interactions between participants and artifacts. The act of organizing and displaying objects gave the students the autonomy to speak

12 Anthropologist Claude Lévi-Strauss defined the 'bricoleur' as one who makes do with institutional and cultural contexts: "he 'speaks' not only with things, as we have already seen, but also through the medium of things: giving an account of his personality and life by the choices he makes between the limited possibilities." Claude Lévi-Strauss, *The Savage Mind* (Chicago: University of Chicago Press, 1966), 21.

"through the medium of things," creating both individual and collective non-verbal narratives.[12] During the exhibition opening, students curated individual gallery talks where they could choose a collection of objects on display to represent their first-year experience. The project allowed the Kharkiv School of Architecture to craft new narratives in real time through the curation of material objects, student experiences, and architectural propositions.

▲ Outpost Office, *Open/Work*, Kharkiv, Ukraine (2019). Photo: Erik Herrmann. Courtesy of Outpost Office.

Architecture's intellectual negotiations between desires and realities are well documented, but an architecture that results *from* negotiation is more difficult to describe. Architects are often managers of favors, masters of bartering, or pawns of politics. As the digital machinations of ecommerce attempt to smooth out the inherent friction between supply and demand, the algorithm has stealthily removed the possibility of the productive misunderstanding or the favorable exchange in face-to-face material procurement. If we consider *blat* as a creative platform, then the space of friction is also the space of invention. The happy accident, the kindness of strangers, peer-to-peer negotiations, material reciprocity, pooled resources, knowledge sharing—these are design frictions akin to program requirements, site conditions, or client desires, and might actually be more consequential to the final design than we realize.

Elements of this text were adapted from an essay previously published in *Dialectic VIII: Subverting – Unmaking Architecture?* edited by Ole Fischer and Michael Abrahamson with feedback from an anonymous peer reviewer.

CULTURAL
FULFILLMENT

REAL ESTATE BUBBLE ARCHITECTURE
Lluís Alexandre Casanovas Blanco

Since 1985, Spain experienced a long-term increase in the economic value of real estate, with the construction industry becoming the strongest economic sector in the country's GDP. For decades, Spain's government and private banks promoted the purchase of property and the construction of housing as the safest investments for the moderately wealthy middle class.[1] As sociologists Isidro López and Emmanuel Rodríguez pointed out, Spain served as "an international laboratory," where the financialization of homeownership operated at a much larger scale than seen in other international markets.[2]

The privileging of housing as the safest investment led to an outburst of suburban development throughout the Spanish territory, significantly modifying its landscape and contributing to the environmental deterioration of some of its regions.[3] Also nicknamed *"boom del ladrillo"* (brick boom), the bubble collapsed in 2007 with the global crisis unleashed by the Lehman Brothers' bankruptcy. This phenomenon left behind a huge housing stock, which reflected the societal transformation of most of the country's population through the consolidation of a credit system and the emergence of diverse financial products. Spanish architects and stakeholders are now faced with the challenge to deal with the material remnants of the boom, undertaking the management of its urban and architectural legacy.[4]

In order to lay out possible modes of architectural intervention, this essay focuses on the series of design strategies developed for the Real Estate Boom House, an early-1990s house that I refurbished in 2018.[5] Though existing analyses of the architectures of the Spanish Real Estate Bubble often disregard the role of developers and contractors, these professionals had unprecedented influence over urban growth and architectural typology. The essay includes excerpts from an in-depth interview with Teófilo Ortega, constructor of a number of houses in the Barcelona region during the 1990s and early 2000s. Ortega was the original "designer" of the Real Estate Boom House, owned by Jaume and Maria Lluïsa. Ortega's experience helps us understand how construction responded to speculation, urbanization, and the general demand for housing tied to the historical forms of leisure associated with natural environments. My intervention in the house sought to establish a dialogue with some of Ortega's strategies.

The original Real Estate Boom House can be considered a manifestation of the aesthetics fostered by this financial phenom-

1 For an accurate analysis of this period, see Isidro López, Emmanuel Rodríguez [*Observatorio Urbano*], *Fin de Ciclo: Financiarización, territorio y sociedad de propietarios en la onda larga del capitalismo hispano (1959-2010)* (Madrid: Traficantes de sueños, 2010); and Raquel Rodríguez Alonso, Mario Espinoza Pino, *De la especulación al derecho a la vivienda.: Más allá de las contradicciones del modelo inmobiliario español* (Madrid: Traficantes de sueños, 2017).
2 Isidro López, Emmanuel Rodríguez, "The Spanish Model," *New Left Review* 69, May-June 2011, *The New Left Review* online, accessed October 16, 2020, https://newleftreview.org/issues/II69/articles/isidro-lopez-emmanuel-rodriguez-the-spanish-model.
3 As Ada Colau, spokesperson for the *Plataforma de Afectados por la Hipoteca* (PAH) [*Platform for People Affected by Mortgages*], explained when she addressed the Spanish Deputy Congress in February 2015, "mortgaging has not been a free option for citizens ... In Spain, everything, absolutely everything, impelled you to buy housing, which is not a whim, but a basic need recognized as a fundamental right ... The State's official message ... was that housing was the safest investment a family could make, that the best thing to do in this country was to buy a home. Therefore, what the population did was exactly what the State told them to do." See the video *Intervención de Ada Colau en el Congreso, El País,* February 6, 2013, accessed October 3, 2020, https://elpais.com/politica/2013/02/06/videos/1360141021_027865.html.
4 Attempts to understand the architecture of this period have mostly revolved around the aesthetics of the unfinished constructions left after the 2008 crisis, theorized under the rubric of ruins. In fact, there has been an attempt to distinguish the "architecture" from the "urbanism" of the period, framing planning as wholly responsible for the boom construction aesthetics. In that regard, see the coincidence of two different exhibitions at the Museo ICO in Madrid, "Spain mon amour," curated by Luis Fernández-Galiano, and "Ruinas modernas," curated by Julia Schulz-Dornburg. See: Natividad Pulido, "Luces y sombras de la arquitectura y el urbanismo." *ABC,* March 19, 2013, accessed October 12, 2020, https://www.abc.es/cultura/arte/20130320/abci-arquitectura-20130319z104.html. On the idea of modern ruins, see the different initiatives by architect Julia Schulz-Dornburg, "Leftovers from the real estate bubble: a database," Julia Schulz-Dornburg, accessed on October 12, 2020, https://www.juliaschulzdornburg.com/leftovers-from-the-real-estate-bubble-a-database?page_id=1208; Julia Schulz-Dornburg, *Ruinas modernas, una topografía de lucro* (Barcelona: Àmbit).
5 This research started prior to the refurbishment of the Real Estate Boom House, commissioned in 2016. I returned and extended some of its findings after the house was completed in 2018. For an analysis of the house, see Camilo García, Diego Barajas, "The Real Estate Boom House." *Assemble Papers,* Issue 10: Housing, 2018: 24-31, expanded online as https://assemblepapers.com.au/2018/10/11/real-estate-boom-house/ 9, accessed October 12, 2018; and Iván López Munuera, "Bellavista Riot." *AN INTERIOR,* Issue 3 (Summer 2018): 46-55.

enon.[6] The house's design, materials, and construction details reveal that the suburban desire to return to the rural is an aristocratic marker underlying much of the Real Estate Bubble design in Spain. These ideals are best expressed in the house's street façade, the crux of which is a medieval-like cylindrical tower enclosing the house's central staircase. Crowned by stepped crenels and pierced by two symmetrical pointed windows, the tower both evokes history and inverts this typology's historically associated function, as its roof is not accessible.

▲   Entrance, Teófilo Ortega's garden, Santa Agnès de Malanyanes. Photo: José Hevia (2018). Courtesy of Lluís Alexandre Casanovas Blanco and José Hevia.

The house is separated from the street by a fenced garden, interrupted by the garage access. To enter, one must pass through a porch supported by two Doric-like, cement columns. The façade's basement is clad in stone sheet, and the upper part is covered by small, white-pearled stones cast into mortar paste. The windows are protected with fencing that contains botanical motifs. Despite these references, the house's interior responds to an orthodox Corbusian *Domino* concrete structure that vertically divides the program into three floors: the ground floor contains the house's communal spaces, including the living room, kitchen, and dining room, as well as access to the backyard garden; the first floor encompasses four bedrooms, connected by a long, central corridor; the second floor consists of a single space, thought of as a studio or working area.

The view from the street contrasts with the house's rear façade, a much more sober design with no decoration. This façade, visible from the town center, was intended to be eventually blocked by the future urbanization of the buffer cornfields at the edge of the neighborhood. In fact, the potential extension of the neighborhood was always meant to obstruct the house's magnificent views of the town center; as several scholars have argued, the Spanish Real Estate Bubble was undergirded by an illusion of limitless growth, which also implied infinite

---

6 The editors of the Australian magazine *Assemble Papers* chose the house to illustrate an interview with Dutch-American sociologist Saskia Sassen. In this interview, Sassen argued that "a building is no longer simply a building. It's been transformed into an asset." According to Sassen, "when you financialize buildings through algorithmic mathematics … the building is still there, yes, but the actual operational event is not the building as such … If you have transformed it via 16 really complex steps into something else, the building is there, but its real functioning is invisible to our eyes." "Saskia Sassen: The Limits of the Material. Words by Jana Pérovic. Images: Real Estate Boom House by Lluís Alexandre Casanovas Blanco." *Assemble Papers*, Issue 10: Housing (2018): 31.

possibilities of urbanization. Tied to the promotion of weekend residences inspired by bourgeois narratives of close-to-nature leisure, the urbanism of the boom devoured the landscape it inserted itself in.

The biography of the house's constructor, Teófilo Ortega, illustrates the transformation of Spain's economic policies since the mid-20th century. Ortega was born to a peasant family in Jaén, Andalusia in 1942. In 1958, a teenage Ortega and his brother left Spain to serve as factory workers for the car manufacturing company Opel, located in Rüsselsheim am Main, in the Federal Republic of Germany. The two brothers migrated in order to hoard enough savings to become homeowners in Spain. "After a year," Teófilo explains, "we had already amassed enough money to do so. We decided to stay a few more years to save enough money to establish our own construction company in Spain."[7] The Ortegas moved back to their home country in December 1963, when the Francoist government approved the first of a series of *Planes de Desarrollo* (Development Plans) that, under the tutelage of the United States, attempted to modernize the country's crippled economy.[8] The success of these policies—known internationally as the "Spanish miracle"—allowed a transition from an antiquated economy based on agriculture to a more competitive industry and a bustling services sector—a phenomenon credited with fueling the emergence of a Spanish middle class.

During the late 1970s, the company founded by the Ortega brothers specialized in the construction of multi-family residential projects in Barcelona. Following the rapid increase of the real estate market throughout the territory after 1985, Teófilo decided to buy a set of five plots in the new Bellavista residential area in Cardedeu, a 30-minute drive from Barcelona. "There were rumors that land property was about to rise," Ortega explains, "and I started looking for plots on sale close to the city."[9] Well-connected to Barcelona via roads and railways, Cardedeu experienced significant urbanization during the late 1980s. Located in a biologic corridor linking the Maresme coastal region and the Montseny hills, this town soon became a privileged holiday destination for the bourgeois urban class emerging at the end of the 19th century. Hygienist movements considered its environment a healthy retreat close enough to the city but far enough away from its toxic air. The widespread adoption of

7 Teófilo Ortega, Conversation with the author, January 20, 2019, Santa Agnès de Malanyanes, Barcelona.
8 The Primer Plan de Desarrollo (1964–1967) was approved by the Law 194/1963 on December 28, 1963, and was adopted in practice on January 1, 1964.

the car led to a regional roundabout system that enabled easier access to Cardedeu from bigger cities. The seasonal variation in the town's population caused a progressive shift in its economy, moving from a dependence on agriculture and stockbreeding at the beginning of the 20th century to a reliance on the service and construction sectors at the start of the 21st century.[10] Conversely, the urbanization of the agricultural landscape around the town's historic center partially deteriorated the town's ecological resources, interfering in its natural hydrography and adding significant stress to some of its autochthonous species.

The Bellavista neighborhood is one of the major residential areas that popped up at Cardedeu's limits during the mid-1980s. Conceived as a segregated area, the neighborhood was secluded from the town by buffer fields and pine forests. The urban fabric of Bellavista was designed as an orthogonal, suburban grid engulfing a few remaining country houses previously devoted to agricultural exploitation. The neighborhood included no services or facilities, further supporting a fantasy of isolation inspired by rural ideals. Most of the houses in Bellavista served as second residences owned by prosperous, middle-class dwellers from Barcelona wishing to spend weekends and summers away from the city and closer to natural environments.

In 1988, Ortega built five houses in a row in the plot at the Bellavista neighborhood, which were quickly sold. With this money, the contractor acquired another five-plot package at the neighborhood's edge, where Jaume and Maria Lluïsa's house would be erected. But this time, Ortega left the plots inactive until 1990. "I bought the plot at a very competitive price," explains Ortega, "when taxes on land were still low. When I decided to use the plot, the market prices had considerably risen, and so did my profit margin. In a way, you could say I speculated with the terrain, but that was not premeditated. I was busy building elsewhere."[11] At the time, Bellavista started attracting a stable residential population who moved there permanently from nearby cities. Ortega defines 1992, when Jaume and Maria Lluïsa bought the house, as "a moment of euphoria."[12] According to the developer, "only a few sensed that the real estate

9 Teófilo Ortega, Conversation with the author.
10 According to data published by the municipality, at present the construction sector represents 17 percent of the town's economy, following the service sector which makes up 38 percent. "Economia," *Ajuntament de Cardedeu*, accessed October 12, 2018, http://www.cardedeu.cat/el-muni cipi/cardedeu/economia/.

Guernica Tower, Teófilo Ortega's garden, Santa Agnès de Malanyanes. Photo: José Hevia (2018). Courtesy of Lluís Alexandre Casanovas Blanco and José Hevia.

Greenhouse, Teófilo Ortega's garden, Santa Agnès de Malanyanes. Photo: José Hevia (2018). Courtesy of Lluís Alexandre Casanovas Blanco and José Hevia.

bubble was about to burst, but the majority of the population was still confident in property being a safe investment."[13]

An architecture aficionado, Ortega developed a marketing-based design method of his own early in his career. "I tried to build spacious houses, with singular construction details I designed myself," Ortega states. "This allowed me to market the houses quite well within a very large housing market pool at the time."[14] Ortega's case is telling: the architecture of his constructions should be explained through the increased value of their details. According to the developer, his aim was "to make something different from the modern barrack that everyone at the time was building, to move away from cookie-cutter houses by offering a different geometry than the cubical constructions appearing all over the country."[15] According to the constructor, "the architects I worked with in the beginning insisted that 'no one will like what you want to build.' But I actually proved them wrong, as sometimes I even sold my houses a week after putting them on sale."[16] Ortega fragmentarily sketched the details he wanted in his houses and then brought them to an architect, who worked on its assemblage while ensuring that everything followed local regulations and codes. In his building process, Ortega explains, "the architect served only as a sort of legal advisor."[17] In charge of the design process, the constructor's architectural dilettantism was supported exclusively by experience. Ortega notes a specific interest in Arabic architecture, examples of which he visited in his childhood in Andalusia.

11 Teófilo Ortega, Conversation with the author.
12 Ibid.
13 Ibid.
14 Ibid.

In discussion of architectural form, Ortega affirms an interest in geometry. "I like to think about architecture as a geometric question, rather than a stylistic one. I like to formulate myself, 'How would I build that in such a rigid land plot?' and then work on it through material experimentation as if I was 'physically' resolving a mathematical problem."[18]

Thus, Ortega acknowledges the invention of pseudo-historical technical details and decoration to singularize a rather banal structural and programmatic configuration. In fact, Ortega's discourse exemplifies one of the main contradictions of the boom in Spain: although it appealed to a sort of return to the rural, its functioning was intimately linked to the destruction of rural spaces and natural environments. According to Ortega, "when building in the city, I would rather use different aesthetic and technical solutions. It is, mainly, a typological question: apartment housing is much more constrained, and its relation to the exterior is limited to strictly regulated facades. On the contrary, houses in the suburbs, as isolated volumes surrounded by garden space, open up the possibility to experiment with geometry and volume."[19]

⋀　Street façade, Bellavista neighborhood, Cardedeu. Photo: Joana Colomar and Nilo Zimmermann. Courtesy of Lluís Alexandre Casanovas Blanco.

A visit to the developer's house in Santa Agnès de Malanyanes, close to Cardedeu, attests to his design method. The house, with a round plan, is surrounded by an ample garden. From the late 1980s to today, the garden served as a laboratory where Ortega tested some of the details that he would implement in his houses. This space appears now filled with remnants and still-standing architectural artifacts, including colorful greenhouses, fountains, basins, sculptures, chimneys, and fences. Their surfaces are mostly covered with Gaudí-inspired "trencadís" mosaic, here repurposed as a figurative technique to represent varied popular imagery, including Picasso's *Guernica* or Catalan nationalist symbols. Presiding over the entrance path that leads to the house door is a scale replica of Norman Foster's Saint Mary's Axe in London, a structure that, Ortega argues, "is to me much more interesting" than the similarly shaped Agbar tower designed by Jean Nouvel in Barcelona.[20]

15　Ibid.
16　Ibid.
17　Ibid.
18　Ibid.

The surroundings of the constructor's house are also porched, echoing the Doric-like cement columns at the entrance of Jaume and Maria Lluïsa's house. In fact, this column could be considered one of Ortega's signature elements, as it can be found in most of the houses the contractor developed from the late 1980s onward. Ortega conceived of this element when working on the first set of row houses in the Bellavista neighborhood in the mid-1980s. The builder conducted a series of experiments in order to determine the column's "optimal geometry, its weight capacity, and the cheapest and fastest process to build it."[21] After a few months, he arrived at a hollow column solution, in which he poured cement into a mold sculpted with a base, a shaft, and a capital. To conserve material and act as a rainwater pipe, the mold contained a polyvinyl pipe reinforced with wire. This process was quite arduous, and the resulting element contained a number of imperfections on what was meant to be a smooth surface. Ortega used a hydraulic hammer to chip the surface of the columns, not only to conceal imperfections, but "so you could feel they were manually done."[22] The constructor held this result in opposition to "the plain, soulless finishes of buildings currently popping up elsewhere."[23] In the absence of technical and scientific means, construction research during the real estate bubble embodied a deskilling of construction processes used for high-standard detailing, appealing instead to an aesthetic discourse that obscured the use of low-quality materials and rough details, as well as a lack of expertise and machinery. Such is the case

⋀   Entrance hall. Lluís Alexandre Casanovas Blanco, *Real Estate Boom House* (2018). Photo: José Hevia. Courtesy of Lluís Alexandre Casanovas Blanco.

19 Ibid.
20 The resemblance between the two buildings was a highly debated matter in the English press but remained quite under-acknowledged in the Spanish one. Jonathan Glancey "Another fine pickle: How Barcelona stole London's prize gherkin - and had the cheek to improve on it." *The Guardian*, March 28, 2005, accessed October 12, 2018, https://www.theguardian.com/artandde sign/2005/mar/28/architecture; Peter Popham, "Architecture: The Gherkin goes global," *The Independent*, October 18, 2005, https://www.independent.co.uk/news/uk/this-britain/architec ture-the-gherkin-goes-global-320365.html.

for the infamous stippled paint technique or *gotelé* (from the French word *gouttelette*, droplet)—referred to as popcorn painting in English—which covers some of the walls in Jaume and Maria Lluïsa's house. As Paula García-Masedo and Andrea González have highlighted, what started as a practice to conceal the lack of success in achieving perfectly smooth gypsum surfaces soon became a marker of sophistication in the decoration of real estate bubble interiors.[24]

After 20 years, the area around the tower-encased staircase was partially covered with mold, and its roof had leaks. Jaume and Maria Lluïsa wanted the top floor to be sectorized in order to control noise and temperature. Thus, I was asked to refurbish the house. The dissection of the above-mentioned processes provided me with design tools to interpret the house's elements as documents proving a connection between economic policies, technical details, and environmental transformations. The refurbishment meant also an opportunity to rethink the evolution and user transformation of the Real Estate Boom architecture.

⌃ View of the interior garden. Lluís Alexandre Casanovas Blanco, *Real Estate Boom House* (2018). Photo: José Hevia. Courtesy of Lluís Alexandre Casanovas Blanco.

This premise translated into a number of material and spatial operations. The clients wanted the *gotelé* to be removed from the walls surrounding the staircase, where humidity had significantly deteriorated their distinctive droplet finish. As I have explained, this technique had a symbolic value that referred to the historical context in which the house was conceived, speaking about the forms and conditions of labor under which the built environment was produced under the Real Estate Bubble. Before removing this finishing per the clients' request, we decided to make a series of casts of the walls' surfaces. These patterns served as a mold to cast a series of transparent poly-

21 Teófilo Ortega, Conversation with the author.
22 Ibid.
23 Ibid.
24 Paula García-Masedo, Andrea González, *Proyecto para recuperación de paredes lisas de galería de arte* (Madrid: Caniche editorial, 2017).

urethane curtains to control the intense Eastern sun streaming through the staircase's pointed windows in the morning. Possible to fold and slide, the opacity and color of these curtains significantly changes during the day, generating different projections of the *gotelé* pattern into the staircase space.

Although the economic value of the now-deserted plots behind the house lost real estate value after the collapse of this economic system in 2008, a much anticipated eventual recovery of the Spanish economy could lead to their urbanization, converting this piece of land into more single-housing fabric. To anticipate this view blockage, the house's views are rethought within its plot limits. The staircase space is therefore filled with a hanging garden, with a design that falls between a traditional *patio cordobés* and the now-ubiquitous vertical garden. Treated as landscape scenography, the direct observation of the staircase space, or its view through windows, simultaneously constructs an alternative view to the rear garden as well as it refers to the encapsulated, artificial nature of the suburban garden. To highlight this aporia, this interior garden is conceived as a highly-technified space. The different species supported by transparent pots are monitored through a series of sensors connected to a computer.[25] This system reports the plants' levels of humidity to a screen as well as the overall air quality of the space, rendering these species as explicitly subdued to a mythic hygienic function.

Ultimately, what are the larger implications of this material dialogue between the architect and the constructor? The understanding of the historic, socio-economic, and political contexts under which the architecture of the original Real Estate Boom House was produced had two important disciplinary effects. On one hand, it unveils how architecture is the product of many agents beyond the professional architect. On the other hand, the context surrounding the built environment proves useful in conceiving new forms of architecture which may expose and remain out of sync from neoliberal narratives. Ultimately, as amateurish and experimental as his construction details are, Ortega's techniques illuminate the alliance between real estate practices and architecture, offering the possibility of disrupting the logics that originally made them possible.

25 The gardening system was envisioned by architects Paula Currás and Álvaro Carrillo. Under the name *Calypsos*, these designers conceived in 2016 a series of interactive filters to manage air quality within domestic and indoor settings. Currás and Carrillo were asked to adapt this system to the Real Estate Boom project.

BLANKETS
Current Interests

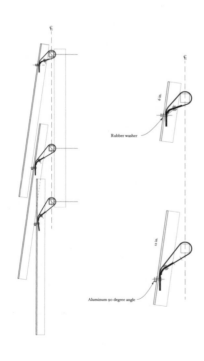

Current Interests, *Silver House Studio* (2019).

On the topic of desire, we think of blankets as systems of comfort and defense. Yes, soft. Yes, submissive. Yes, tolerant. These highly constructed substrates do some badass work. Consider the following: solar blankets, insulation blankets, sound blankets, packing blankets, retention blankets, lead blankets, security blankets, anxiety blankets, electric blankets, homeless blankets, wet blankets, quilted blankets, woven blankets, felted blankets, baby blankets, accent blankets, car blankets, beach blankets, lightweight blankets, heavy blankets, nappy blankets, messy blankets, cozy blankets, silky blankets.

In these images, two projects sit side by side. One is a building proposal for an artist studio with stacked and hung corrugated concrete shingles, dyed dark and extra dark. We call this project *Silver House Studio* (2019), named after the small house existing on the site with lap siding painted a car-primer silver. Layers of pigment, cladding, tinted glass, rubber, steel frame, blanket insulation, columns, and column covers come together and dampen the signals between exterior and interior. Alongside this project are images of *Rough Coat* (2018), a set of façade-scaled blankets exhibited in a gallery, painted dark and dimly lit. The work is panelized, tailored, quilted, stuffed, tufted, sewed, snapped, draped, painted, and sprayed with stucco. Moving between these tectonically excessive projects are latent thoughts of presence, sidedness, privacy, and desire.

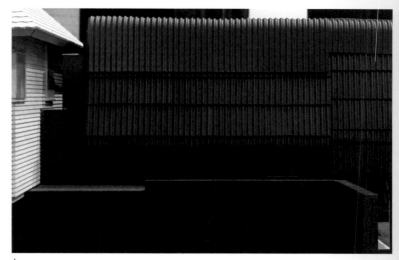

▲   Current Interests, *Silver House Studio* (2019). Photo: Michael Vahrenwald.

▲   Current Interests, *Rough Coat* (2018). Photo: Joshua White.

∧ Current Interests, *Silver House Studio* (2019). Photo: Michael Vahrenwald.

Current Interests, *Rough Coat* (2018). Photo: Tia Thompson.

Current Interests, *Rough Coat* (2018). Photo: Tia Thompson.

Current Interests, *Rough Coat* (2018). Photo: Joshua White.

Current Interests, *Silver House Studio* (2019). Photo:
Current Interests.

THE ARCHITECTURE OF DESIRE: AN ESSAY IN VI TANGOS[1]
Cristina Goberna Pesudo

Our appetite for production is never enough.

We live in a culture where the speed of consumption makes it difficult to digest, let alone contest, anything.

With resistance out of the way, architecture becomes increasingly nicer, kinder, more polished, comfortable, surely more salable, with less shadows, less corners, less doubts, less risk.

A clean, polite architecture, all positivism and optimization.

An ideal that architectural education has too often cheerily followed.

Paradoxically, desire is defined as almost the perfect antithesis of that, as it is all about a dangerous otherness.

May these words serve as fragments for a recuperation of an Architecture of Desire.

I: The End

Desire is the end of reason, a notorious little death, or a death straight.

Death is associated with tears, and sometimes the sexual act is associated with laughter.

But laughter is not so much the contrary of tears, just as tears are not so much the contrary of ecstasy most of the time.

In her book *Not One Day,* the OuLiPo's first female member and writer extraordinaire Anne Garréta describes a collection of women, unfolding 12 stories where the flashing fragility of desire shines as something alive, autonomous, and wayward.[2] Where beauty is drawn as both, a retroactive elegy and a death, announced.

An Architecture of Desire by definition is always aware of its end.

But the end of architecture never seems to be contemplated, as its decay and destruction are historical taboos.

Cristina Goberna Pesudo, "Suite Tokyoite," *The Book of Sins: Lust* (2018).

"When will a Pritzker prize be given for the elimination of a building?" Keller Easterling asks in her book *Subtraction*, quoting A. P. Leeuven who lines up a number of built works that he assures share high and similar heights of bad taste.[3]

Gordon Matta Clark's work *Office Baroque* was commissioned in 1977 by the International Cultural Centre in Antwerp to carry out a project in an empty office building, which he consequently proceeded to cut. In an interview published for the exhibition catalog, he explains how he received many positive letters about his piece. The angry ones, though, were penned by architects. One claimed that he had violated the building's dignity by transitioning it to ruin or demolition; others accused him of holding an ideological position that was perfectly opposite to the role of the professional architect and everything related to solving human problems.

Desire raises a tsunami of dilemmas.
And the Architecture of Desire never solves problems.

1 Tango: Interaction marked by a lack of straightforwardness. Something that, like desire, you have to dance to the end.
2 Anne F.Garréta, *Not One Day,* translated from the French by Emma Ramadan. Deep Vellum Press, 2017.
3 Keller Easterling, *Subtraction*, Sternberg Press, Critical Spatial Practice 4, Berlin, 2014.

II: Unreason

Our appetite for reason is also never enough.

Searching for an end raises desire and by definition defies reason.

The ultimate end of desire, as of love, is its rationalization.

As Slavoj Žižek claims, if you know why you love someone, then you surely don't really love them.

An Architecture of Desire rejects reason.

For their '67 graduation Diplôme Collectif, the Parisian group A. J. Aérolande, founded by Jean Aubert, Jean-Paul Jungman, and Antoine Stinco, submitted an inflatable at the École de Beaux-Arts, an institution that measured quality by the degree of mastery of neoclassicism and adjacent styles.

The inflatable in question not only defied the heavy structures of Beaux-Arts architecture, but also its representation. It was based in unreason: As a premise it was going to be rejected, as it was a projection toward an uncertain architectural future we did not yet have the means to build.

It was pure Architecture of Desire.

Λ Cristina Goberna Pesudo, "Suite Tokyoite," *The Book of Sins: Lust* (2018).

III: Seduction

The most sexual part of sex is not about gratification but about anticipation.

The Architecture of Desire is a promise, a striptease in the making, erotism versus pornography, a field of exploration and a land of discovery, the foresight of worlds yet to come, of societies yet to arrive.

Architecture is, historically, a dream of dreams, nightmares incorporated.

Seduction is the opposite of what pornography offers. Pornographic language doesn't play but communicates information instead. Pornography destroys desire in a more efficient manner than repression.

Seduction versus pornography operates within architecture as the difference between a vibrant space for citizens, as opposed to a perfect area for consumption; the difference between an agora and a mall; the difference between an architec-

Λ Cristina Goberna Pesudo, "Suite Tokyoite," *The Book of Sins: Lust* (2018).

tural representation of immediate consumption and one that causes estrangement.

An architecture that delivers its message straight and unveils a core perfectly aligned with an agenda that has no mystery, no seduction, no suggestion involved, will be a pornographic operation.

The perfect opposite of an Architecture of Desire.

⋏ Cristina Goberna Pesudo, "Suite Tokyoite," *The Book of Sins: Lust* (2018).

IV: Imperfection

From iPhones to Brazilian wax, from corporate architecture to millennial pink design, everything seems to be wrapped in a glow of polished familiar perfection.

In his book *Saving Beauty*, Byung Chul-Han explains how polished objects don't hurt, nor do they offer any resistance. All negativity and otherness is eliminated.
　　As he illustrates it, Jeff Koons is the master of polished surfaces. Andy Warhol loved a beautifully clean surface, too, but his work is still charged with negativity and death.
　　But Jeff Koons's works are not Trojan Horses—they do not hide anything.
　　The world of clean, clear surfaces lacks wounds and guilt, but also skills in the old art of seduction.

In a wound there is something poignant, something that moves you, as opposed to the effect created by objects of soft perfection. Polished things are all positivism and optimization, maybe like most corporate architecture, the kind that proliferates in financial districts, brands our cities, and hosts global empires. The kind of architecture that presupposes a permanent growth and does not align with imperfection.

V: Dirt

Pleasure is the ultimate rebellion.

In architecture, pleasure and hedonism have been accused of frivolity by politically engaged agendas, and of vagueness or uselessness by neoliberal ones.
　　But the object of desire is often a little broken, capturing our heart because of its visible, challenging vulnerability and imperfection.

Desire has nothing to do with the fast

achievement of pleasure.

Desire has nothing to do with soft, clean, nice, kind beauty and its easy, rapid consumption.

Desire is based in the other's otherness: It is dangerous, it has shadows, it is pure resistance, it is not convenient or pragmatic.

Desire is pure risk, something that could blow you away or destroy you, and probably will do both. Making architecture desirable again is to challenge its polish, its comfort, its complacent beauty.

Along those lines, maybe the only possible relationship with architecture today is a criminal one, understanding the criminal not as an outlaw, but as a fugitive from the logic of perfection, easy consumption, and the market of ideas and things, the market of architectural education and the construction of cities.

Maybe, instead, we should vindicate architecture as a privileged space for risk.

VI: Strategies for an Architecture of Desire

Strategies for an Architecture of Desire is a piece that offers a variation of a famous work by Brian Eno, which was used in the creative process of recording David Bowie's *Berlin* album trilogy. It is a set of cards that rejects originality, offering strategies that, if not necessarily in a straight or oblique fashion, will give you suggestions to turn your designs into something:

A little Imperfect
Somehow Dirty

Pure Architecture of Desire.

> Set of cards. Cristina Goberna Pesudo, *Strategies for an Architecture of Desire* (2020).

UNMARKED GRIEF: THE INSTITUTION OF SILENCE
The Destitute Institute

The period between 1936 and 1945—that is, the Spanish Civil War and its aftermath—is known as the White Terror, a time during which thousands of people were killed and buried in ditches and fields.

With the death of fascist dictator Francisco Franco in 1975, Spain started a process toward the democratization of its institutions of power. At the country's first free referendum in 1978, a democratic constitution was passed. This gaze to the future also meant covering up its violent past—a pact of silence about victims and killers still remains.

Meanwhile, only 700 mass graves out of 3,000 have been exhumed.

The film *Unmarked Grief: The Institution of Silence* (The Destitute Institute, 2020) investigates the fate of those assassins, whose crimes have fallen into a forgiving silence. All except for one: José Lluis Vilallonga—aristocrat, playboy, international actor, and writer—who was part of a firing squad on the fascist side of the Spanish Civil War. This film recalls Vilallonga's memory of the events, as described in his memoirs, which are illustrated by a series of images from *Architects' Data* by Ernst Neufert, a polemical volume widely used in architectural schools but with a Nazi-related past.

The project has a three-fold mission: to understand the soil as the repository of the memory of unsolved murders; to draw and define the veiled side of the institution that put obstacles in place to obstruct solving the crimes; and to involve a younger generation of Spaniards in the film's production (a voiceover actress and pianist), who have lived in the pact of silence over a generation lost.

The Destitute Institute Presents
Unmarked Grief: The Institution of Silence

An idea by Albert Fuentes, Cristina Goberna and R.O alias Rubén Ortega
Written and devised by Cristina Goberna and Albert Fuentes

Text: José Luis de Vilallonga, read by Judit Calvo Lethem (13 years old)
Music: Erik Satie, "Vexations" played by Maia Fuentes (15 years old)
Images: Ernst Neufert's *Architects' Data* (1936), edited by Cristina Goberna,
Preliminary Report on the Exhumation of a Mass Grave from the Spanish Civil War
in Puerto Real (Spain) by Jesús Román Román and Juan Manuel Guijo Mauri (2015),
Jeanne Moreau and José Luis de Vilallonga in Louis Malle, *Les Amants* (1958).

1936

I remember that on the first night I was sent to a country house where the officers lived. There was a boorish but funny officer who brought me a cup of coffee with milk at 5 a.m., telling me to drink it in one shot. It was pure liquor with a bit of coffee. I was not used to drinking so I went to execute prisoners at sunrise heavily drunk. I can't recall well what happened. I just remember that there was lots of noise.

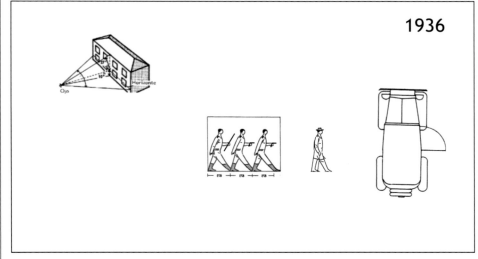

1936

Men in shooting squads were given a huge cup of cognac in the morning. Those folks would volunteer only for the cognac … because the first day it is horrific, the second one too, the third one a bit less, and by the eighth you do it as if you were killing hens or rabbits.

1936

I arrived with a Basque friend of my age who was named something like Olazabal. Upon joining the squad, he had a hysterical laughing attack … and there he is … still laughing in a sanatorium.

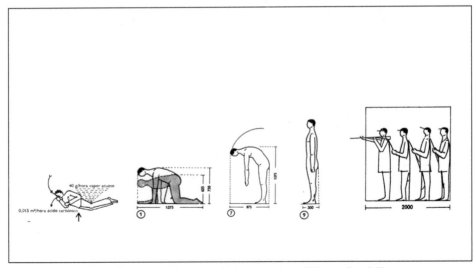

Cinematographic shootings have nothing to do with real rifle snaps. People do not die with dignity. They fall down like potato sacks. Reality is banal and completely unheroic. The death of someone shot by a firing squad lacks pride, he falls like a hallucinated imbecile.

*I understood Germans much later. Those savageries were done out of lack
of responsibility. If you are lifted from responsibility you become
a beast. You do what you are told and you get used to it, period.*

*There are still nights that I wake up thinking like those people who
suffer nightmares that never leave. I have talked about it with a couple
of friends who are psychiatrists. They said … man … these are things
that mark you for life. Get used to it because nobody will tell you that
they'll go away. No, they never will. The terrible thing is not to kill,
but to become a clerk of death.*

EXHIBITION: FULFILLED

IF IT FITS, IT SHIPS®
Ashley Bigham

In February 2020, I curated the *Fulfilled* exhibition at the Banvard Gallery to coincide with the eponymous symposium at the Knowlton School of Architecture.[1]

For the exhibition, I asked 40 designers to submit contents for storage and display with the only requirement that the submission arrive in a standard USPS Priority Mail Large Flat Rate Box. The gallery was offsite storage, organized around a row of stacked IKEA shelves held together with industrial polyester strapping and fitted with motion-activated LED tube lights: each box's contents would be on display for the duration of the exhibition. These contents would be stored in the gallery for one month, free of charge, before they were returned to the sender. There was no request to create new content for this exhibition, although some did. The designers' responses included self-published books, models of sand movement in Singapore, camouflage slippers from an exhibition in South Korea, flat-rate boxes inside flat-rate boxes inside flat-rate boxes, façade material samples, rotting fruit, tiny suburban houses, an invoice billing me for time and labor, a hair clip and button-down shirt, a box which needed to be hand delivered due to the failings of international customs agents, and various other miscellaneous architectural ephemera. The exhibition design explores the aesthetic potential of industrial storage typologies. As a prompt and a physical installation, *Fulfilled* was an opportunity to explore modes of architectural practice that rely on negotiated authorship of objects, systems, and designers.

No doubt, many designers recall the glass sculptures Walead Beshty created from 2005-14 by shipping glass sculptures in FedEx boxes to galleries across the country only to reveal the harsh reality of their transit when they arrived with various shatter patterns. For Beshty, the final form of the object was acquired through its movement. In contrast to Beshty's approach, many *Fulfilled* designers approached the design of their objects as commercial fulfillment often does, with the goal to appear effortless. Each designer must have imagined the physical forces that their box might encounter during transit and considered the likely resilience or possible destruction of their contents.

Authorship over the condition of the box and its contents was conceded, at least in some part, to the United States Postal Service. In many instances, this became part of the design process itself. Bureau Spectacular's submission came in the form of two EPS foam pieces— an object and its packaging, or two architectural models—depending on how you choose to interpret them. On the other hand, Future Firm designed packaging for a bag of water from Lake Michigan, the contents of which, if not properly secured, could dissolve into the cardboard itself. Several other submissions provide contents that offer little distinction between packaging material and architectural representation: Keith Krumwiede's green tissue paper under suburban home models; Dylan Krueger's fine excelsior wood shavings bunched around a white model; Curtis Roth's CNC-milled foam insert containing a ream of paper, scissors, tape, and a single invoice billing me for his time; or Ang Li's reclaimed EPS-foam objects shrink wrapped to fit the 12" x 12" x 6" box interior.

The submissions generally fit into three categories: those who used the box for storage/transportation of miscellaneous materials related to their creative practice (Common Accounts, MOS, The LADG, and Besler & Sons); designs that focused on the particularities of the box itself as a medium (Amelyn Ng, Medium Office, and Spinagu); and designs that utilized the constraints of the flat-rate logistical system while projecting architectural objects unrelated to the medium itself (Office III, Office Kovacs, and T8projects).

In *The Ecological Thought*, Timothy Morton coined the term "hyperobject" to describe objects that are "distributed in time and

1 The *Fulfilled* exhibition was designed by Outpost Office, a collaboration between Erik Herrmann and me.

space relative to humans."[2] Architect Clare Lyster has made the comparison between Morton's "hyperobjects" and logistical architecture along with their accompanying physical objects including the cardboard box, server, fiber-optic cable, barcode, delivery truck, and credit card.[3] Given these parameters, we might consider the postal service itself as a hyperobject. As with many "invisible" fulfillment networks, the value of the postal service often feels intangible. We are familiar with its objects (trucks, envelopes, mail boxes) but struggle to articulate its spatial impacts. The USPS is a vast spatial phenomenon whose very success (the invisibility of its network) makes its failure in a capitalist system possible.[4] It is, to use Morton's words, a "complex situation that is uncanny and intimate at the same time."[5] As one of the oldest public utilities (and the only one which is hand-delivered daily into one's domestic space), this "uncanny and intimate" system makes it unique among fulfillment networks, which often attempt to be either completely invisible or wholly discernible.

USPS Priority Mail Flat Rate Boxes debuted on November 20, 2004 and, according to the USPS, immediately began "delighting consumers with their simplicity and convenience, attracting business shippers with an impressive value proposition, and confounding competitors attempting to match their ability to reach virtually every address in the nation."[6] At approximately 12" x 12" x 6", the Large Flat Rate Box is easily carried by a single human.[7] It stacks effortlessly. Its ratio is a pleasing 2:2:1. Its dimensions, weight allowances, and delivery time have been honed to fit within the existing network of USPS logistics.

With the rise of online shopping, the box as a material object has become the stand-in for the physicality of the shopping experience. Instead of consistently embracing this ease, however, we often seek out the friction of the physical shopping experience within the

2 Timothy Morton, *Hyperobjects: Philosophy and Ecology after the End of the World* (Minneapolis: University of Minnesota Press, 2013).

3 Clare Lyster, "Territories of Equivalence: Objects of the Logistical Apparatus," *Footprint* 12, no. 2, ed. Negar Sanaan Bensi and Francesco Marullo, (Autumn/Winter 2018): 25-36, https://doi.org/10.7480/footprint.12.2. (Ana Miljački also refers to Timothy Morton's hyperobjects in the introduction of this book).

4 See Jacob Bogage, "White House rejects bailout for U.S. Postal Service battered by coronavirus," *The Washington Post*, April 11, 2020, https://www.washingtonpost.com/business/2020/04/11/post-office-bailout-trump/.

5 Timothy Morton, "Poisoned Ground: Art and Philosophy in the Time of Hyperobjects," *symplokē* 21, no. 1-2 (2013): 43.

6 United States Postal Service, "Postal Service Priority Mail Flat Rate Boxes Celebrate Birthday," news release no. 10-112, November 18, 2010, https://about.usps.com/news/national-releases/2010/pr10_112.pdf.

digital supply stream. For example, online unboxing videos highlight the excitement associated with shopping by capturing the moment of the first physical resistance. These videos describe every aspect of the material unboxing experience from the texture and color of the box to the design of the object's packaging. In this version of shopping, the initial moment of material interaction with the object and its container happens in the comfort of one's own home or, increasingly, within a makeshift home studio. The practice of filming the unboxing process is one which caught on with hobbyists, amateur fashion icons, kid celebrities, and tech bros sometime around 2006, coinciding with the growth of ecommerce and the need for companies to create an emotional dimension for the at-home shopping experience.[8]

As *Fulfilled* boxes poured in from across the country, including a few that traversed oceans or crossed international borders, we set out to document the discovery of each box's contents in the style of a YouTube unboxing video. Hired actors faithfully opened each box and shared their immediate, unscripted reactions and descriptions of the contents. In front of a bright-yellow background, the actors attempted a series of improvisational characters, often mirroring their own online personalities. Thus, the unboxing video (as a cinematic experience and a physical form stored on YouTube's servers) becomes yet another multifaceted artifact of global distribution chains, a translation of a fleeting, emotional experience into a finite, representational medium. However, the physical or representational gap between an object, its packaging, and its environment, is a space of profound cultural production. As the anthropologist Anna Lowenhaupt Tsing writes in her book, *Friction: An Ethnography of Global Connection*:

> the closer we look at the commodity
> chain, the more every step—even
> transportation—can be seen as an
> arena of cultural production. Global
> capitalism is made in the friction in
> these chains as divergent cultural
> economies are linked, often

7 The official size of the box is 12 1/4" × 12 1/4" × 6" and can weigh up to 70 lbs for the flat rate of $21.10.
8 "Unboxing," Wikipedia, last modified September 05, 2020, https://en.wikipedia.org/wiki/Unboxing#:~:text=Yahoo%20Tech%20places%20the%20first,on%20gadgets%20or%2 ofashion%20items.
9 Anna Lowenhaupt Tsing, *Friction: An Ethnography of Global Connection* (Princeton: Princeton University Press, 2005), 51.

awkwardly. Yet the commodity must emerge as if untouched by this friction.[9]

Can a logistical system share authorship with a curator? In the case of the United States Postal Service, maybe it can. I consider *Fulfilled* to be a large collaborative design project among a curator, 40 architectural practices and their numerous designers, Outpost Office, a graphic designer, a group of student actors, the United States Postal Service, The Ohio State University's email service, the servers at Instagram and YouTube, Lowe's, and IKEA. The exhibition uses the constraints of economics, logistics, and communication networks to produce difference through the friction naturally occurring between these individual systems, each with its own built-in biases, efficiencies, and, of course, inefficiencies. It is important to recognize this contemporary mode of practice, in which cultural and logistical fulfillment issues are treated equally in the design process to shape the production of the work *and* also the conception of its form. While most shipping experiences work hard to appear effortless, *Fulfilled* allows the frictions within the transportation system to not just become visible, but to become an active agent in the design process itself. In *Fulfilled*, friction is design.

⋏ Film still from unboxing videos, *Fulfilled* (2020). Courtesy of Outpost Office.

AMELYN NG

ANG LI

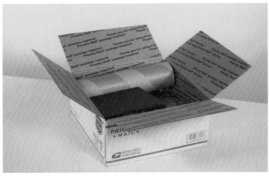

A/P PRACTICE

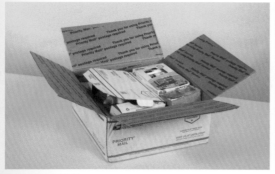

BESLER & SONS

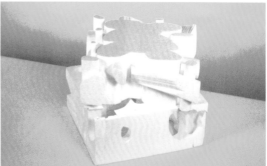

BUREAU SPECTACULAR

COMMON ACCOUNTS

CRISTINA GOBERNA PESUDO

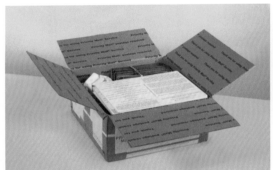

CURRENT INTERESTS

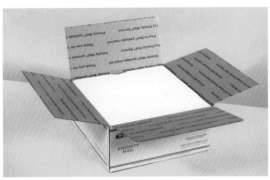

CURTIS ROTH

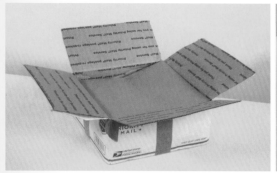

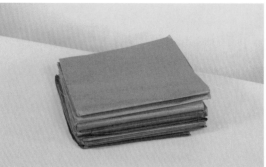

D.ESK

DYLAN KRUEGER

ESTHER CHOI

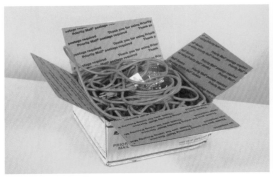 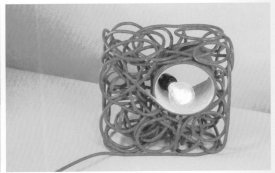

EXTENTS

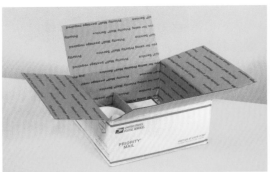 

FORMLESSFINDER

FUTURE FIRM

FULFILLED EXHIBITION

GALEN PARDEE

HOME-OFFICE

JACK SELF

JESSE LECAVALIER

KEITH KRUMWIEDE

 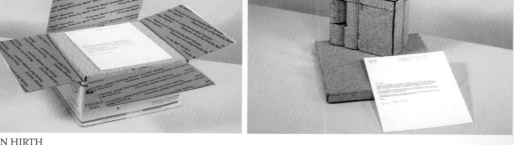

KEVIN HIRTH

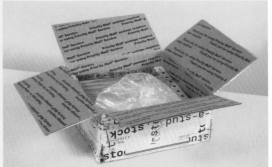

LAIDA AGUIRRE

LEIGHA DENNIS

LLUÍS ALEXANDRE CASANOVAS BLANCO

MEDIUM OFFICE

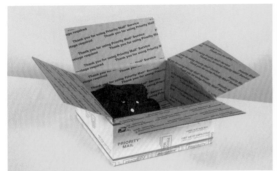

MICHELLE JAJA CHANG

MOS

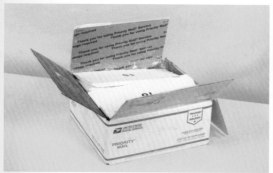 

NEW AFFILIATES

OFFICE III

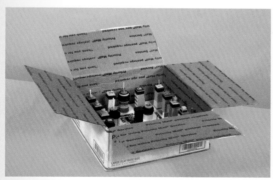 

OFFICE KOVACS

SPINAGU STUDIO

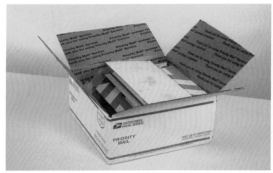 

STUDIO BARNES

T+E+A+M

FULFILLED EXHIBITION

T8 PROJECTS

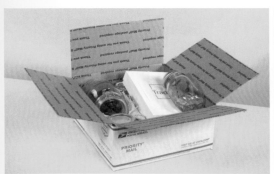 

TAMEKA SIMS

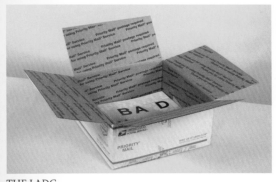 

THE LADG

THE OPEN WORKSHOP

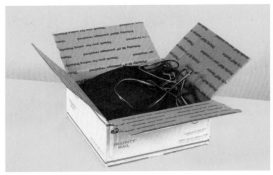

TONY GONZALEZ

ZACH COHEN

 Fulfilled (2020). Photo: Erik Herrmann. Courtesy of Outpost Office.

▲ *Fulfilled* (2020). Photo: Erik Herrmann. Courtesy of Outpost Office.

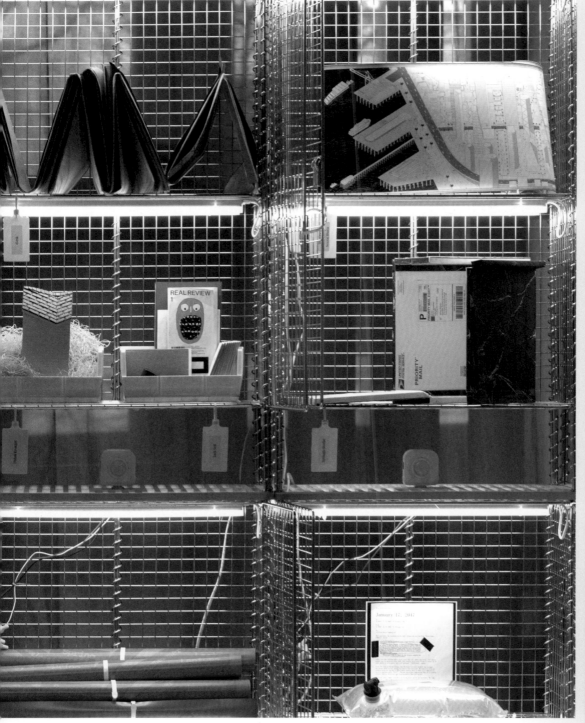

Fulfilled (2020). Photo: Erik Herrmann. Courtesy of Outpost Office.

⋏ *Fulfilled* (2020). Photo: Erik Herrmann. Courtesy of Outpost Office.

∧ *Fulfilled* (2020). Photo: Philip Arnold. Courtesy of Knowlton School.

⋏ *Fulfilled* (2020). Photo: Erik Herrmann. Courtesy of Outpost Office.

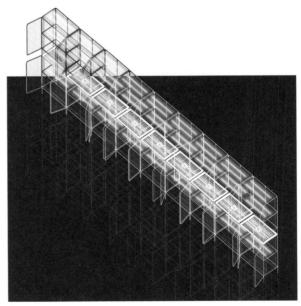

⋏   Drawing of stacked storage units, *Fulfilled* (2020). Courtesy of Outpost Office.

∧ *Fulfilled* (2020). Photo: Philip Arnold. Courtesy of Knowlton School.

ʌ   *Fulfilled* (2020). Photo: Erik Herrmann. Courtesy of Outpost Office.

RETURNED
John McMorrough

I gave a letter to the postman; He put it in his sack.
Bright and early next morning; He brought my letter back.
—Elvis Presley

Fulfilled, an ideal state, rendered as the elision of execution and emotion, characterizes the promise of contemporary delivery, transportation from one place to another (from A to B) and from one state to another (from potential to plenitude). As a conveyance by which to see contemporary architectural production, it is, as most such conceits are, both illuminating and obscure, analogizing the premise as demonstration of proof (means are the ends) by way of the ingenious curation of readdressing content (the end is the means). This volume argues that our world, and by extension our architecture, is subject to, and a subject of, delivery.

The collection shows the range and robustness of the metaphor is imminently architectural—involving forms and functions, containers, and contents—but the work featured herein comes from, and goes to, as many different ontologies as there are packages in a UPS truck. Some of these are projects as products (reified entities constructed out of the excesses of extensive supply chains), some are containers (vectorial accommodations of quantities in their metrical distribution), and others are logistical (multivalent nexus of virtual networks and physical navigation). The overlapping of shared interests posited as a reflection on contemporary multinational package delivery offers both an object of study and an embodiment of contemporary existence, a speculative possibility for locating the purchase, the architectural, or the self as a specific (if not unique) presence as an object addressed (given a singular identity), as well as temporality as a subject accounted for (related to a schedule). As a set, the collection represents a change in attention from the image of commodity to the stuff-ness of an already fully commodified world, a paradigmatic shift away from packaging to packing.

The delivery of architectural content through the context of delivery, that was the idea. But from the initiation of this volume as a symposium and exhibition in the winter of 2020 to the writing of this afterword in the winter of 2021, everything has changed (who knows what the state of things will be by the time you read this). In the interim, the transmission of content (architectural and otherwise), the ostensible theme of this volume, has become, for lack of a better term, complicated. The hermeneutical intricacies of content (signification, allusion, metaphor) and address (to audiences both self-selected and pre-screened), as the usual concerns of academic proceedings, have been superseded by the urgency of exigency. Supply chains new and old are in peril, and the very possibility of delivery of any kind is in question. The US Postal Service operates under the specter of imminent collapse, and yet, we order absolutely everything from Amazon (all the while wondering if its deliveries are pulsing with viral infection). To say nothing of those with orders not delivered because there is a mistaken address, it is lost in transit, or it was never fulfilled in the first place. Delivery has never been more necessary or more precarious; architecture finds itself in a parallel position, simultaneously necessary and precarious.

One of the realizations of being subject to the systems of distribution management *in extremis* is that the conclusion of a transaction is not necessarily the delivery, but in some special cases, the return. In the refusal of acceptance, the return is the procedural manifestation of a misalignment between expectation and realization. The return is not strictly a failure; it is a disappointment (of frustrated consummation) and a delay (the postponement of gratification), but also, in the wider consideration, it is a continuation of potential (the "right one" is still out there).

The return has a special place in architecture—ubiquitous, but also relatively unacknowledged. How many proposals, schemes, plans, and propositions have been returned? Most of them? All of them in one way or another? In the realm of consumer culture, the return has two meanings: reciprocal relations of the same term. The return in the first instance is the refusal of goods (whatever the offering, product, plan, or project). In the second valence, the response to the return is to make another attempt at acceptance in a new and improved version. The cultural logic of the avant-garde (itself a return, returned to again and again) is to deploy, retreat, reassemble, and remount. Considered under this established model of returns, the efforts of this volume represent an attempted correction in the conception of design as differentiated attempts to get it right, while at the same time, at least tacitly understanding that the results will be only more returns (and in turn, continuing the Project of projects).

However, the simplified mechanical *fort/da* model of returns has been superseded by a realization that a return need not return. Using Amazon.com as an example (is it still an example when their map has become our territory?), their process of returns shows how the categories of refusal and repetition have become extended and inverted. Starting with the decision to return an item, the first step is indicating the reason for the return. The possible responses given are extensive (bought by mistake, does not fit, the wrong color) while also insignificant (as it states, "your response will not affect your return"). The means of return are similarly asignifying. Sometimes you can send it back for free, sometimes at a cost. Sometimes you print a label to send the item back in the box it came in, other times you may be asked to drop it off, *au naturale*, with only a QR code on your phone. Sometimes you are instructed to leave it with a reasonable parcel entity (like USPS or UPS) and other times at a random locale connected only by some corporate arrangement (Whole Foods, sure, but Kohls?). On some lucky occasions you are even told not to bother to send it back, the thing itself is acknowledged to be worth less than the effort the return requires. Regardless of shipping method, the return is not going back to the warehouse to be restocked (a return to origins, to enact the cycle again); it is off to a facility so that it can be sold en masse with whatever other random array of items fits on a pallet to a reseller. The return is no longer a sending back, but a sending on, not an end, but a beginning.

What are the possibilities for fulfillment amidst this extended field of return? Perhaps one way of thinking about the exchange and overlap would be to characterize design as this form of exchange without culmination, not as accumulation, but as distribution. Not as a repository, a dead letter office scrap heap of previous attempts, but as a recurrent continuum of elements and assemblages, a Pandora's box of consequences never completed. Fulfillment comes, like the wish of the monkey's paw, in ways we do not expect. The return, in this sense, is not strictly a nullification, but an extension, a continuation of potential, cycled again and again, not as something recycled, but as a possession in the space between receiving and returning—communal ownership via refusal. The labels may be worn off, though one can still read "architecture" (or maybe it reads as "design" by this point). The postage due for the ideal of such transportation is not its achievement, but its engagement, the state in which we are all, at least for the moment, *Fulfilled*.

ACKNOWLEDGMENTS

I am grateful for the institutional support provided by The Ohio State University, the Knowlton School of Architecture, and the Institute for Materials Research. At the Knowlton School, Todd Gannon encouraged this project from its inception and provided key institutional resources. Karen Lewis and Jennifer Clark graciously moderated portions of the symposium. IKEA generously provided material support to the *Fulfilled* exhibition with the donation of a discontinued storage system and a reception of meatballs and lingonberry punch.

This book would not exist without the editorial skills of Sarah Rafson and Candace Opper of Point Line Projects and the brilliant graphic design of Ingrid Chen. Several OSU students were instrumental in the construction of the *Fulfilled* exhibition including Eleanor Lewis, Faith Martin, and Caroline Kerka. I am especially thankful for the support I received from the Graham Foundation for Advanced Studies in the Fine Arts. MacDowell provided me invaluable time and a beautiful space to complete this project.

A special thanks to the participants of the symposium who shared their time and intelligence; I am privileged to call them co-authors of this book. And to the participants of the *Fulfilled* exhibition who blindly joined my experiment with generosity and wit, you have my enduring gratitude.

I would like to thank John McMorrough for his continual support, intellectual insight, and sustained curiosity and Julia, Matthew, and Walter for keeping us all grounded in 2020. Thanks to Keith Krumwiede who provided the keynote lecture and spectacular fictions of suburbia, which have inspired my interest in fulfillment and the American dream. Ana Miljački's generosity and political provocations continue to infuse this project with the richness of hope, in all its complexities. Although not directly involved with this book, I can't imagine pursuing the topic of fulfillment if not for the enduring influence of Keller Easterling, an inspiring presence from my time at Yale.

And finally, no single person was as instrumental to this work as Erik Herrmann, a constant joy and inspiration who makes all my best works possible.

Published by Applied Research and Design Publishing, an imprint of ORO Editions.
Gordon Goff: Publisher

www.appliedresearchanddesign.com
info@appliedresearchanddesign.com

Editor: Ashley Bigham
Copyediting: Point Line Projects
Book Design: Ingrid Chen
Project Manager: Jake Anderson

10 9 8 7 6 5 4 3 2 1 First Edition

ISBN: 978-1-951541-64-4

Color Separations and Printing: ORO Group Ltd.
Printed in China.

AR+D Publishing makes a continuous effort to minimize the overall carbon footprint of its
publications. As part of this goal, AR+D, in association with Global ReLeaf, arranges to plant
trees to replace those used in the manufacturing of the paper produced for its books. Global
ReLeaf is an international campaign run by American Forests, one of the world's oldest non-
profit conservation organizations. Global ReLeaf is American Forests' education and action
program that helps individuals, organizations, agencies, and corporations improve the local
and global environment by planting and caring for trees.